The Australian Flag

The First 100 Years

GEOFF HOCKING

The Five Mile Press

The Five Mile Press

The Five Mile Press Pty Ltd
22 Summit Road Noble Park
Victoria 3174 Australia

Phone: +61 3 9790 5000
Fax:　　+61 3 9790 6888
Email: publishing@fivemile.com.au

First published 2002
Printed in China

Text © Geoff Hocking

All rights reserved

Designed by Geoff Hocking
Edited by Emma Borghesi

Printed in China

NATIONAL LIBRARY OF AUSTRALIA
CATALOGING-IN-PUBLICATION DATA

Hocking, Geoff
The Australian flag: the first 100 years.
ISBN 1 86503 599 8.

1. Flags – Australia – Pictorial works.
2. Flags – Australia – History. I. Title.
929.920994

RIGHT:
*Dawn at ANZAC Cove, Gallipoli,
ANZAC Day, 25 April 2001.*

(Photograph courtesy Australian Associated Press)

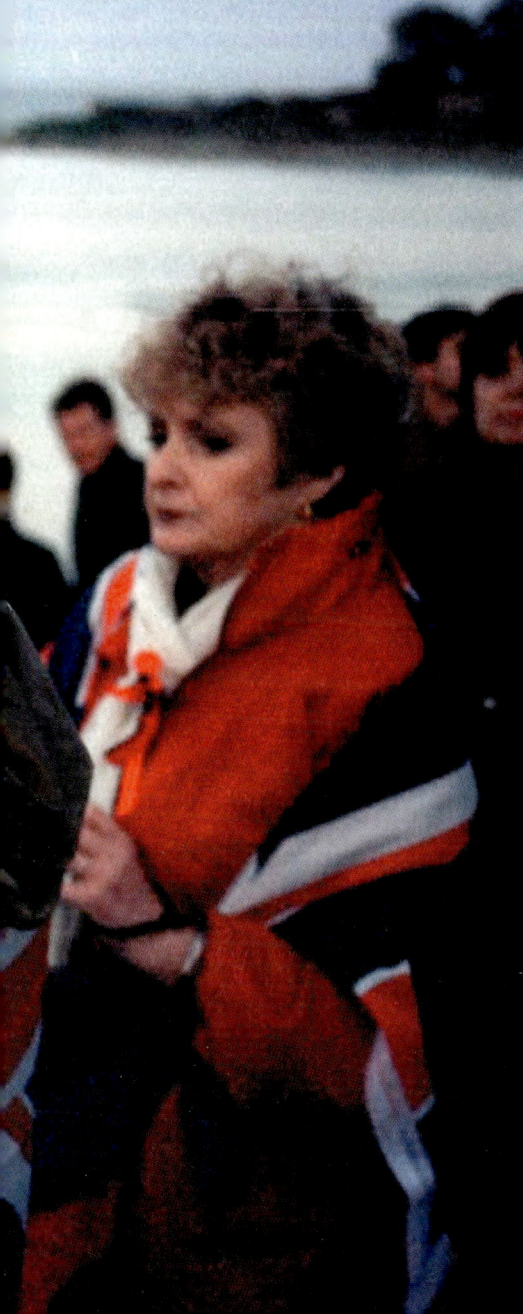

The Australian Flag ~ The First 100 Years

CONTENTS

Introduction 5

Chronology of Flag Design 6

Advance Australia Fair 7

Terra Nullius 20

Whose Country? Which Flag? 43

Rally Behind Which Flag? 57

Just for Fun 79

Aussie! Aussie! Aussie! 90

Flags of the Nation 99
   The Union Flag and the Union Jack 100
   The Australian National Flags 102
   Flags of the States 104
   The Aboriginal Flag 106
   Flags of the Territories 106
   Flags of the Services 108
   New Ideas! 109
   Flag Protocol 110

Index 112

RIGHT:
Andrew Gaze carries the flag into Stadium Australia at the opening of the Sydney Olympic Games 2002.

(Photograph by Steve Christo, courtesy of the Melbourne Age newspaper)

The Australian Flag ~ The First 100 Years

LEFT:
Advance Australia Coat of Arms, c. 1901.

(Courtesy Rex Nan Kivell Collection, National Library of Australia)

ABOVE:
Come On Boys. Follow The Flag!
World War I recruiting poster by Robert Northfield. Printed by Troedel and Cooper, Melbourne, c. 1915.

This call to arms and rally behind the flag is typical of the messages understood by most Australians.

The flag is British, but at the time most Australians believed themselves to be Britons and the defence of the mother country was a natural extension of the patriotism felt for their colonial home.

It was not until 1971 that Australians ceased to be British subjects and earned the birthright to be Australian Citizens.

(Courtesy Rex Nan Kivell Collection, National Library of Australia)

INTRODUCTION

The first attempt by one early colonist to create a new design for a symbolic flag for Australia was as far back as 1806 when a New South Wales squatter took his wife's silk wedding dress and fashioned a banner in honour of Nelson's victory at Waterloo. John Bowman's flag featured both the kangaroo and the emu standing on either side of a shield decorated with the more traditional symbols of the British Empire, the rose, the thistle and the shamrock.

Bowman had created a design which embodied the essence of the flag that is flown by all Australians almost two centuries later, with the symbol of Britain combined with the symbol of Australia's unique place in the world — the Union Jack combined with the Southern Cross.

There are, however, many who dispute the relevance of the symbol of that foreign land on the Australian national flag as the country enters its third century, now freed of those political and colonial ties that bind.

There is no doubt that history and tradition are powerful ties that continue to bind Australia emotionally to the United Kingdom but there are many other forces that demand that the young nation create its own unique mark to show to the world. There are also those who believe that 'Brand Australia' needs to be able to market itself without confusion to the rest of the world. In the global marketplace Australia may still seem more like a branch office than a unique entity able to stand on its own.

It is this argument that fuels the constant debate in Australia over what the Australian flag could be. Can tradition be set aside in favour of a new vision for an independent nation? It seems that, in Australia, polarized political persuasion will always get in the way of national unity. The Australian hatred of class distinction, and the derision of 'tall poppies' and social elites will always disavow informed opinion; a scant regard for authority scoffs at political leadership and the ongoing war between the classes will continue to devalue the most popular symbol of all.

While Australians continue to agree on reasons to disagree they will continue to present themselves to the world in a confused manner, with a confusing array of symbols, flags and colours: green and gold; red, white and blue; black, red and gold; kangaroo, emu, stars and crosses.

Australians all unite . . . !

Chronology of Flag Design

29 April 1770 — Captain James Cook planted the Union Flag of Great Britain at Botany Bay, on the Australian east coast, the first raising of an English flag on Australian soil.

22 August 1770 — Cook sailed north along the coast, until, on an island off Cape York, he again raised the flag, claiming all of the eastern coast of Australia as New South Wales, for the British Empire.

26 January 1788 — Captain Arthur Phillip arrived at Botany Bay in command of the first fleet of 11 ships, 700 convicts, 70 troops and officers.

1806 — New South Wales squatter, John Bowman, created a flag made from his wife's wedding dress which featured a kangaroo and emu beside a shield decorated with an English rose, Scotch thistle and Irish shamrock. It was the first use of Australian fauna on a symbolic or heraldic design.

1823 — Two naval officers, captains Nicholson and Bingle, produced their design for a National Colonial Flag for Australia. Based on the British naval ensign with the stars of the Southern Cross placed upon the cross of St. George, this flag received support from the Lords of the Admiralty but gained little local favour.

1851 — A flag closely resembling the present Australian flag, embroidered with the words 'Australasian League Tasmania', was unfurled in Van Diemen's Land. This flag, known as the anti-transportation flag, heralded the end of transportation of convicts to the colonies in 1853.

August 1853 — Discontented gold-diggers march on the government camp, behind the 'Diggers Flag', on the Bendigo goldfields.

December 1854 — In Ballarat on the Victorian goldfields, a group of diggers angered by persistent ill-treatment and corruption by police and officials, rallied beneath the flag of the 'Southern Cross', a white, five-starred cross set on a brilliant blue ground.

1867 — It is believed that the 'Australian Federation League' flag was first displayed at a function held in Melbourne to honour Prince Alfred, Australia's first royal visitor. Most expected this attractive and popular design would be adopted as the first flag of the federated colonies, but sadly, this was never to be.

November 1900 — The Melbourne newspaper, the *Review of Reviews*, in conjunction with the federal government offered a prize for a design for a new national flag. Five entrants submitted almost identical designs and jointly shared in the glory.

3rd September 1901 — Prime Minister Edmund Barton unveiled the new National Ensign for Australia at the Exhibition Building in Melbourne.

28 February 1903 — After two years, King Edward VII finally signed the papers that officially recognized the new Australian flag. A blue ensign, with the Union Jack in the upper left corner and the stars of the Southern Cross in the fly was to become the government flag. The federation star, a large six-pointed star, sat directly beneath the Union Jack.

A red version (red ensign) was approved for civil use and for merchant shipping.

Both flags saw some slight changes in design over the next few years.

1954 — The *Flags Act* of 1954 officially confirmed that the blue Australian flag was the 'National Flag'. Prior to this Act, the blue flag was called the 'Australian Ensign'.

12 July 1971 — The 'Aboriginal Flag', designed by Arrante artist Harold Thomas, was flown for the first time on National Aboriginal and Islander Day in Adelaide. This striking red, yellow and black flag has since been recognized as one of the many official Australian flags.

1983 — The 'Boxing Kangaroo' flag became the unofficial sporting flag of the nation after Perth businessman Allan Bond took it to glory when his mega-yacht *Australia II* beat all comers and brought home the America's Cup.

3rd September 1996 — The National Flag was proclaimed to commemorate the first raising of Australia's National Ensign/Flag.

26 January 1998 — The *Age* and the *Sydney Morning Herald* newspapers held yet another competition for the design of a new flag for Australia. Again there were thousands of entries. As Australia neared the end of its second century clear choices were being suggested by the designs: the colours of red, blue and gold were predominant, and kangaroos and the Southern Cross also featured strongly.

The Union Jack was rarely to be seen amongst these designs which overwhelmingly refer to the uniqueness of place, peoples and flora and fauna.

ADVANCE AUSTRALIA FAIR

ABOVE:
Australian War Service House Flag.
This flag shows the Union Jack with a King George medal over it and the Southern Cross in the fly.
The words for 'King and Country' read in the white trimmed border.
This paper flag printed by John Sands, Sydney, was issued by the Centre for Soldiers' Wives and Mothers in 1917.
(Courtesy National Library of Australia)

Whether slapping against a pole, flapping in the breeze, or held high in the hands of schoolchildren lining a parade, the flag of the nation is the symbol that ties its citizens together in one community. It is the tie that binds all members of the tribe, one to another.

For all that we hold dear to ourselves as individuals, when we hear that clarion call we do leave behind our daily grind and rally behind our flag. That fluttering piece of coloured cloth, silhouetted against the sky, carries our common aspirations; it can rally us to join together in a common cause; it can lift our hearts and our spirits to achieve feats of unusual courage, of valour, selflessness and superhuman effort.

But what poet ever sang the glory of the Australian flag? What songs have been sung that revere that piece of cloth?

Most countries honour their standard by attaching affectionate 'nick-names' to their proudly fluttering national symbols.

Names such as 'Old Glory', 'Union Jack', 'Maple leaf', 'Rising Sun', 'Star of David', 'Cedars of Lebanon' and 'Hammer and Sickle' all bind the citizens together to the visual symbol that embodies the common aspiration of their nation. But what name do we Australians have for ours? And which of the many flags that are held high by Australians do we honour most?

The night sky over the great south land lights up with a constant reminder to all Australians of their place on the face of the earth. The crooked constellation that is dubbed the Southern Cross has long been held with great affection in the hearts of all Australians.

The lights of the Southern Cross point the way to the south, to the antipodes, where everything is upside down down under.

Mark Twain, the American writer who passed through Australia in 1865, remarked of this curious phenomenon: 'The Southern Cross is ingeniously named, for it looks just as a cross would if it looked like something else'.

While it is reasonable to suggest that the words 'Southern Cross' are held in great affection by most Australians, that name was hijacked by a group of political opportunists on the Ballarat goldfields long before the same stars were ever attached to the Union Jack, and that same symbol has been taken up again and again as a badge of protest by many other political groups in the 150 years since the fateful battle at the Eureka Stockade.

The Australian Flag ~ The First 100 Years

RIGHT:
Masthead of the Advance Australia *journal, 15 July 1907.*

Ever unto the next generations those same stars were held in great esteem, and, by the same token, were held by many with open and hostile resentment.

While the stars of the Southern Cross do form a rallying symbol for Australians, these same words can also divide the nation. Whilst most Aussies acknowledge that the flag first flown at Ballarat in the summer of 1854 is still one of the prettiest of all standards to ever have graced our skies, the symbol itself has been soured by political events, both then and now.

It is a matter of much discussion, hot debate, and at times open resentment amongst Aussies that the Australian flag, that red, white and blue cloth, emblazoned with its six stars, is not unique, nor is it even remarkable. The flag of Australia's nearest neighbour, the land of the long white cloud (New Zealand), is almost indistinguishable from the Australian flag. Whereas the Aussie flag has stars of white, the Kiwi flag has stars filled with red. In both cases, the Union Jack of the 'mother country' dominates in the upper left corner. There are other nations around the world, former colonies all, who share a similar design: the British Ensign modified with localized symbols.

It is a fact, accompanied by a certain amount of embarrassment, that even during the long and divisive Australian republican debate of 1999 the Australian monarchists movement (a conservative group who insistently espoused the retention of the constitutional monarch and the Union Jack in pride of place on the flag), showed a New Zealand flag fluttering on its own website. After some wags in the republican movement gleefully offered this information to the media, the red-starred flag was quickly replaced by the white, but the credibility of the argument was lost.

Kerry Jones, Executive Director, Australians for a Constitutional Monarchy, added to the confusion, and no doubt gave her opponents much pleasure, when she offered her praise for the current flag: 'The Australian flag is, I believe, the best in the world. The seven-pointer (*sic*) star symbolizes our federation of six states and several territories. Our geographic position in the world is shown by the stars of the Milky Way.'[1]

1. The *Sunday Age,* 20 August 2000.

OPPOSITE:
The Subscription Ball, Ballarat.
Watercolour by S.T. Gill, c. 1853.

Born in England, the son of a Devonshire Baptist minister and schoolmaster, Samuel Thomas Gill migrated to South Australia in 1839.

Gill was one of the most prolific artists of the early colonial period. He travelled to the Colony of Victoria after the discovery of gold there in 1851.

This watercolour opposite shows a ball on the Ballarat diggings where successful miners and their partners came together to eat, drink and make merry and celebrate their own good fortune on those rich goldfields.

The 'Stars and Stripes' of America and the 'Union Jack' of Britain are the only flags in evidence in this drawing, but the growing desire for a separate Australian identity is shown in the banner hung from the orchestra stall.

An early design of the Australian crest, the 'Advance Australia' banner complete with emu and kangaroo, is displayed here. Even the early colonists were conscious of the need to define their new home, honouring it with appropriate symbols.

(Courtesy La Trobe Library, State Library of Victoria)

The Australian Flag ~ The First 100 Years

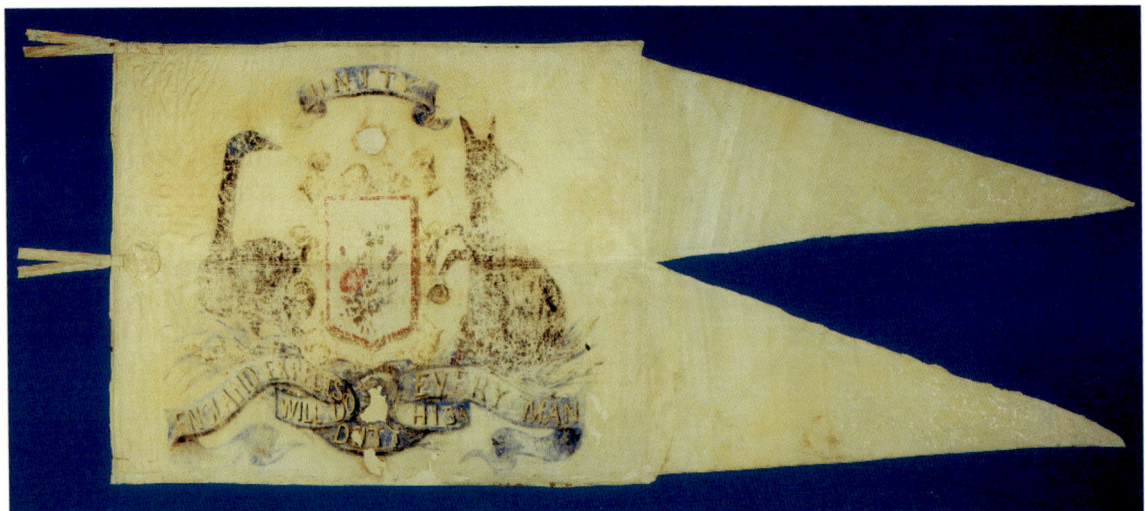

It is just as well that Captain Cook wasn't navigating by Jones' constellation when sailing the southern ocean two hundred years ago.

The Australian flag has been at the centre of debate for the past quarter of a century. Ever since Britain joined the European Economic Community, and Gough Whitlam's Australian government declared Australian citizens were subjects of 'the wide-brown land' and no longer of 'Old Blighty', Australians have questioned the relevance of a national flag which also bears the symbol of a foreign country.

Although the Australian National Ensign first entered service upon federation in 1901, and was proclaimed in 1903 and again in 1909 in

ABOVE:
Collectable card, c. 1901.

The reverse bears the legend 'No1. The Birth of a Nation. A series of 50. Hoadley's Chocolates Ltd'.

(Author's Collection)

LEFT:
The Bowman Flag, 1806.

Inspired by Nelson's victory in the battle of Trafalgar, a squatter from Richmond, New South Wales, John Bowman, created the first flag to be designed in Australia from a remnant of his wife's silk wedding dress.

The Bowman flag features the English rose, Scotch thistle and Irish shamrock, with the first recorded use of a device so familiar to Australians today — the kangaroo and emu standing either side of the shield. The banner at the top of the design carries the motto 'Unity', the first recorded unification of British and Australian symbols.

*(Courtesy Mitchell Library,
State Library of New South Wales)*

OPPOSITE:
The Burial of Burke.
Oil on canvas by William Strutt, 1911.

The body of Australia's greatest colonial hero, the Irish-born Robert O'Hara Burke, wrapped in the Union Jack, is lowered into a grave in the sandy creek-flats by Cooper's Creek in 1861.

The bodies of both Burke and Wills were later exhumed and carried to Melbourne where they received a funeral fit for heroes on 21 January 1863.

So much of Australia's colonial history is touched with the reflected glory of Britain, while conversely many colonists were desperate to make their own mark, and to stamp that proudly with Australian imagery.

(Courtesy La Trobe Library, State Library of Victoria)

Advance Australia Fair

the Commonwealth gazettes, it was not until 1953 that it was officially confirmed as the national flag of Australia. Even with that short history debate has raged amongst conservatives and republicans, those of British descent and those not, amongst new migrants and the oldest inhabitants of the land, young and old, revolutionaries and unionists, students and bushmen, sports fanatics and popstars. The issue of the symbolic relevance of the Australian flag to contemporary Australian society has never dissipated – except for ten days in September 2000, when the fittest and fastest from all the world over descended on Sydney for the Olympics. It was then that the heart of every Australian was filled to bursting with pride whenever 'old whats-its-name' was run up accompanied by the strains of 'Advance Australia Fair'.

The only slight embarrassment possible was if a Kiwi took a medal alongside an Aussie, with the two flags being almost indistinguishable from each other.

After Cathy Freeman carried the spirit of the nation across the finish line of Stadium Australia, she draped her victorious shoulders with both the flag of her country and the flag of the Aboriginal people. And all those who claimed this young native Australian as one of their own at that moment cheered all those sentiments she symbolized. The Southern Cross was entwined with the black, red and yellow of the Aboriginal flag, and in the background thousands of boxing kangaroos fluttered against a sea of green and gold, proclaiming to the rest of the world that this was the modern Australian nation.

Above:
Australia's Hope-Sydney's Pride.
This flag was created by the colonial squatter William Charles Wentworth and Dr. William Bland, who campaigned as a team in the New South Wales parliamentary elections of New South Wales in 1853.

This decoratively embellished white silk flag has a white star below the Union Jack and a red star at the right.

(Courtesy Mitchell Library, State Library of New South Wales)

Advance Australia Fair

ABOVE:
Christmas card, c. 1904.
This card has the following text featured inside:
   Beneath the Flag of this Land so free,
   Long may these States united be.
   A Combination when that Flag's Unfurled
   To Bid Defiance —
   To The Whole Wide World.

(Private Collection)

ABOVE:
A group of boy scouts pose with their leader before their annotated flag.
  The flag bears the name 'Inniskilling', and it is believed that the troop is from Swan Hill in Victoria, c. 1925.

(Courtesy La Trobe Library, State Library of Victoria)

The Australian Flag ~ The First 100 Years

Advance Australia Fair

ABOVE:

Several members of the Matthews family pose on the verandah at Brimpaen.

A young patriot, Bill Brown, holds a flag on a stick in this photograph taken towards the end of World War I.

(Courtesy La Trobe Library, State Library of Victoria)

RIGHT:

Rabbiters' campsite in the bush, c. 1914.

Even after a decade of federation, there are many whose patriotism to the 'King' can deny acceptance of 'Country'.

(Courtesy La Trobe Library, State Library of Victoria)

OPPOSITE:

An artesian bore is sunk at Charlecotes, near Sale in Victoria, c. 1855.

A variation on the popular flags of the day celebrates the success of the bore as water streams away from the pipe.

(Photograph by Frederick Cornell, c. 1855-66. Courtesy La Trobe Library, State Library of Victoria)

Red, white and blue; black yellow and red; green and gold: the colours of the nation, almost a rainbow, for that is really who we Australians are. We are a bit of everything, a little bit of all nations, a mongrel breed as yet still not sure which bit to leave out, which bit to put in, and which colours, traditions and symbols to embrace. How can we bring it all together and include everybody's aspirations without hurting anyone's feelings?

George Brown, a 17-year-old dancer from Wreck Bay on the southern New South Wales coast, was one of hundreds of Aboriginal artists who participated in the opening ceremony of the Sydney Olympics. He recalled the spirit of reconciliation expressed at the games:

I couldn't believe how many non-indigenous people were holding up Aboriginal flags, and the Australian flag with the Union Jack cut out and replaced by the Aboriginal flag . . . that was amazing'.

A new Australian flag may never be accepted because we will probably never make up our minds. In this debate it is the Southern Cross that remains the one constant element that does appeal to us all; it has been a constant symbol throughout all our history.

Although the Union Jack is a symbol that has been with us since the landing of Captain Cook in 1770, its relevance is not enjoyed by many in the country today. While some proudly display bumper stickers which demand we should keep the Australian National Flag as 'our flag forever' others carry the Southern Cross of the Eureka flag as a symbol of defiance—or as a constant reminder to others that it is never too late for change.

As we celebrate a century of change, the change from direct rule from the other side of the world towards an increasing sense of our own identity and a move towards a united, independent nation, it may be time to reassess those images which are used to symbolize our nation and express our aspirations.

LEFT:
Runner Cathy Freeman wins her 400-metre race at the Sydney Olympic Games, 2000.

Cathy carried the hopes of two cultures and one Australian nation across the line, and then ran a victory lap with the Aboriginal and Australian flags tied together, much to the delight of the 100 000 Aussies in the stadium.

After witnessing the fireworks on Sydney Harbour Bridge light up a spectacular federation motif on New Years Eve 2000–01, the following opinion was offered to Sydney readers:

Cathy Freeman need never run with two flags again. Our new national flag was unveiled last night. Roll on the republic!
– Terry Hanly, Annandale New South Wales. Letter to the Editor, The *Sydney Morning Herald*, 2 January 2001.

(Courtesy the Melbourne Age newspaper)

Advance Australia Fair

RIGHT:
Fancy dress and national costume, Melbourne federation celebrations, 1901.

In this group of school children gathered before the photographer in honour of Australia's federation there is no reference at all to the indigenous population of the new nation.

Britannia stands central to this group, with the Union Jack unfurled behind, with 'young Australia' at her right hand.

The Welsh and the Scots are well represented, along with a colonial governor and a 'jolly jack-tar', but the Irish and the Aboriginal are conspicuous in their absence.

The flag of the nation is nowhere to be seen, but young Australia does have a curiously clever construction that holds the cross high.

Australia has taken the best part of the 20th century to break down all of these old barriers born of strife, intolerance, religious differences and jealousies. While the people themselves seem eager to reconcile the whole nation, there does not seem to be the political will to succeed.

Britannia's apron strings bind deeply the will of the conservatives who espouse freedom of the individual yet do their best to thwart anyone who wants to act freely.

(Courtesy National Library of Australia)

LEFT:
Cartoon by Ron Tanberg
(Courtesy the Sydney Morning Herald, *11 October 2000*)

In the words of one anonymous poet:
Our flag bears the stars that blaze at night,
  In our southern sky of blue,
And that little old flag in the corner,
  That's part of our heritage too.
It's for the English, the Scots and the Irish,
  Who were sent to the end of the earth,
The rogues and the schemers and dreamers,
  Who gave Australia its birth.
And you who are shouting to change it,
  You don't seem to understand,
It's the flag of our laws and language,
  Not the flag of a faraway land.
There are plenty of people who'll tell you,
  How when Europe was plunged into night,
The little old flag in the corner,
  Was their symbol of freedom and light.
It don't mean we owe our allegiance,
  To a forgotten imperial dream,
We've the stars to show where we're going
  And the old flag to show where we've been.
It's only an old piece of bunting,
  It's only an old coloured rag,
But there are thousands who died for its honour,
And fell in defence of our flag.
  – ROBIN NORTHOVER

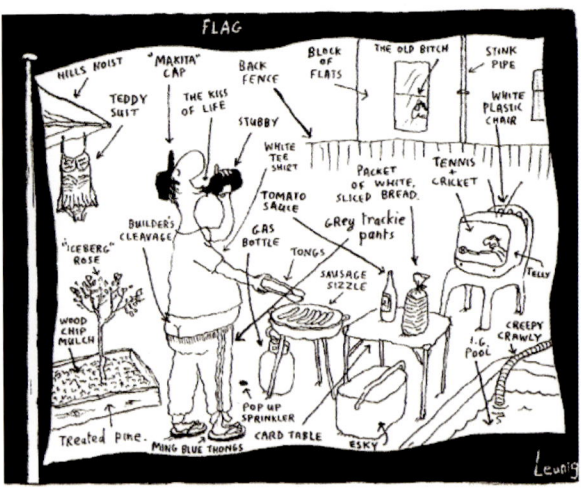

This is the voice of one poet, who like most Australians makes fun of that which he reveres the most. By dismissing his sentiment with the term 'old coloured rag' he gives the flag the greatest of back-handed compliments, and ties the flag of England into our affections by reminding us that many of us are descended from rogues and schemers, cast away from the old country onto these golden shores to forge a new future beneath the southern sun.

But our flag should not be the flag of kings and queens from a foreign land; rather, it should be a flag for the dreamers – dreaming – this new southern land, free to live out that dream beneath the stars of the Southern Cross.

LEFT AND OPPOSITE:
Cartoons by Michael Leunig.
Melbourne based artist and social commentator Michael Leunig is one of those 'rogues' and 'dreamers' who diligently 'pokes a big stick' at the pretensions of contemporary Australian society.

The cartoon opposite, published in the Melbourne Age during the heat of one of Australia's many debates on the issue of a new flag, showed his suggestion for the new design: Leunig offered a flag made of corrugated iron.

He assured Australians that they had all fought under the flag, some even died under it, with his drawing depicting a family at war — in the kitchen — with the flag standing stiffly from a pole on the roof, and a derelict character lying deceased beneath a sheet of iron in the bush.

It seems that fighting and dying under the flag is central to conservatives' objections to any change in the design at all—and Leunig will never let a quirky idea slip him by.

(Courtesy Michael Leunig and the Melbourne Age *newspaper)*

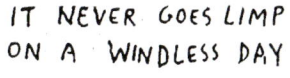

Terra Nullius

(The Land Belonging to No One)

When James Cook first landed on Australia's shores on 29 April 1770, he planted the first British Union Flag at Botany Bay. Cook then followed the east coast until he landed on an island off Cape York, which he called Possession Island. Here, on 22 August, he again raised the Union Flag. With this simple flag-raising ceremony Cook symbolically took possession of the whole of the east coast of the continent in the name of King George III.

It was eighteen years later when Governor Phillip again raised the Union Flag on 26 January 1788 at Sydney Cove, upon his arrival with the first fleet. It was this fleet that carried the shackled convicts, the rogues, schemers and dreamers who helped give modern Australia its birth.

The flag raised at that time was not the British flag we recognize today; it carried only the red cross of St. George (the flag of England) and the white diagonal cross of St. Andrew (the flag of Scotland), which had been added to the St. George banner by Royal Proclamation on 12 April 1606. This was known as the Union Flag or 'Queen Anne' Flag. The diagonal cross of St. Patrick was added in 1801, after which the Union Flag was also known as the Union Jack. The 'Union' celebrates the combination of the standards of the three patron saints of the 'unified' nations that are the British people: England, Scotland and Ireland.

Left:
The landing of Captain Cook at Botany Bay, 1770.
Oil on canvas by E. Phillips Fox, 1901-02.
Painted at the time of Australia's federation this work shows the artist Phillips Fox had certainly done his homework.
(Courtesy National Gallery of Victoria)

Opposite:
Captain Cook taking possession of the Australian continent on behalf of the British Crown, 1770, under the name of New South Wales.
Published in the *Illustrated Sydney News, December 1865.*
In this engraving which commemorates Cook's landing at Botany Bay on 29 April 1770, the artist has made at least one fundamental error.

The flag flying at left bears three crosses: the crosses of St. George, St. Andrew and St. Patrick. However the cross of St. Patrick was not added to the British Union Flag until 1801, after which the flag was known as the Union Jack.

This inaccurate illustration does however foreshadow the designs for several later Australian flags. The White Ensign was adapted many times to the National Colonial Flag of 1823 (which saw the stars of the Southern Cross added to the red cross of the ensign, *see page 26*), the New South Wales Ensign in 1831 and the Federation Flag in 1867 *(see page 27)*, which all popularized the notion of an independent design for a national Australian flag.

(Courtesy National Library of Australia)

The Proclamation of South Australia, 1836.
Oil on canvas by Charles Hill, c. 1856-76.

South Australia was settled quite differently to the other colonies. There had been attempts at mass-migration of free settlers to help develop the fertile country around what is today the charming city of Adelaide.

South Australia had no convict stain, but drew to its shores hard-working Europeans and entrepreneurial Englishmen eager to carve out a slice of the colony.

The Union Jack is about to be flown here for the first time, proclaiming South Australia to be a truly 'English' colony.

(Courtesy Art Gallery of South Australia)

The Proclamation of South Australia 1836.
Charles Hill, Australia 1824-1915
c. 1856-76 Adelaide
oil on canvas, 133.3 x 274.3 cm
Art Gallery of South Australia, Adelaide
Morgan Thomas Bequest Fund 1936.

Terra Nullius

RIGHT:
The Australasian Anti-Transportation League Flag (1851).

The British government had discussed the notion of the federation of Australian colonies as far back as 1849. The Privy Council recommended that the Port Phillip district be granted separation from New South Wales and that Australia be governed by a governor-general and a general assembly with the power to legislate on 'specific matters of inter-colonial interest'.

The bill granting partial self-government to New South Wales in 1850 was passed but the federation clauses proved so contentious that the British government described the move as 'premature' and abandoned the idea.

Not everybody in Australia was pleased with the result and when the Anti-Transportation League was formed in 1851 the colonies rose as one. A meeting of colonialists was held in Melbourne, and one Tasmanian newspaper commented enthusiastically that: 'The league is a great idea. Divided the colonies are nothing—United they are invincible.'

The banner of the Anti-Transportation League is very similar to the present National Flag of Australia, its Southern Cross attempted to bring together all Australians in a common cause (except the colony known as Western Australia which was still eager to receive an imprisoned labour force).

The first steps towards federation had been taken.

(Courtesy Queen Victoria Museum, Launceston)

Twelve feet by nine (4 x 3 metres), this impressive, now almost transparent, silk flag has a yellow Southern Cross in the fly which in 1851 represented the colonies of New South Wales, South Australia, Tasmania, Victoria and — New Zealand.

This design, not at all dissimilar to the flag adopted half a century later, became largely irrelevant after only a few years as transportation of convicts to the colonies ceased in 1853.

New Zealand also declined to join the federation.

23

The cross of St. George dominates the cross of St. Andrew, which in turn supplants the cross of St. Patrick. This design of the Union Jack remains a constant reminder to the 'defeated' nations of the superiority of the English nation.

It was this constant reminder of their homeland far away across the seas, a homeland from where many were banished with the words 'never to return', that tied the hearts of the new 'Australians' to the sunlit outpost of the British empire that Australia was to remain for almost the next 200 years.

In 1823 Captain Nicholson RN and fellow seafarer Captain John Bingle were the first to design what they named a 'National Colonial Flag for Australia'. Their design was based on a white flag with the red cross of St. George and a star in each arm of the cross. The stars were said to symbolize the southern hemisphere 'beneath the Southern Cross'. The design was sent to the Lords of the Admiralty from whom it received official approval; however, this 'National Australian Flag' received little recognition from the ordinary citizens who complained that it was too English, ignoring the Scots and the Irish, who together made up a large and influential number in the population of the colonies.

LEFT:

The Ceremony Unveiling the Statue of Captain Cook, Hyde Park, Sydney (1879).
Coloured Lithograph Supplement to the Illustrated Sydney News, *22 March 1879.*

Almost 100 000 people attended the unveiling of colonial sculptor Thomas Woolner's statue in Hyde Park on 25 February 1879.

The park was decorated with flags and bunting among which are some designs that seem so familiar to us today.

The style adopted by the federation movement is evident in two of those shown. The flag eventually adopted by the Australian nation appears to be an amalgam of many flags already acceptable to the Australian community well before the design competition was mooted.

It was 'the father of federation', Henry Parkes, who commissioned the sculpture from Woolner.

Parkes had an enormous influence over the early colonies; his remarks on Asian immigration did little to calm the fervour of the diggers on the New South Wales goldfields and resulted in the attacks on the Chinese at Lambing Flat near Young in 1861.

The diggers marched into the Chinese camp beneath a flag adapted from the Eureka Southern Cross *(see page 47)* sweeping all before them. This action, in turn, led to the establishment of the White Australia Policy, a much misused and racist policy which took almost another century to be abolished.

(Private Collection)

RIGHT:

Ticket to the Advance Australia League Federal Demonstration, 1899.

The Federation Flag seemed to have been readily accepted and the design promoted to such an extent it seems incredible that it was never adopted as the national flag.

It may be its close resemblence to the flag of the Colony of New South Wales that prompted the other colonies to take a fresh look for the national symbol.

Although federalists were to be found in all former colonies it does seem that Sydney and New South Wales did attempt to exert a lot of influence over the rest of the country.

It may also be that the imperial powers were not interested in a flag that bore any resemblance to that rebel flag flown once at Ballarat and wanted a standard which referred strongly to its own existing designs.

(Courtesy Mitchell Library, State Library of New South Wales)

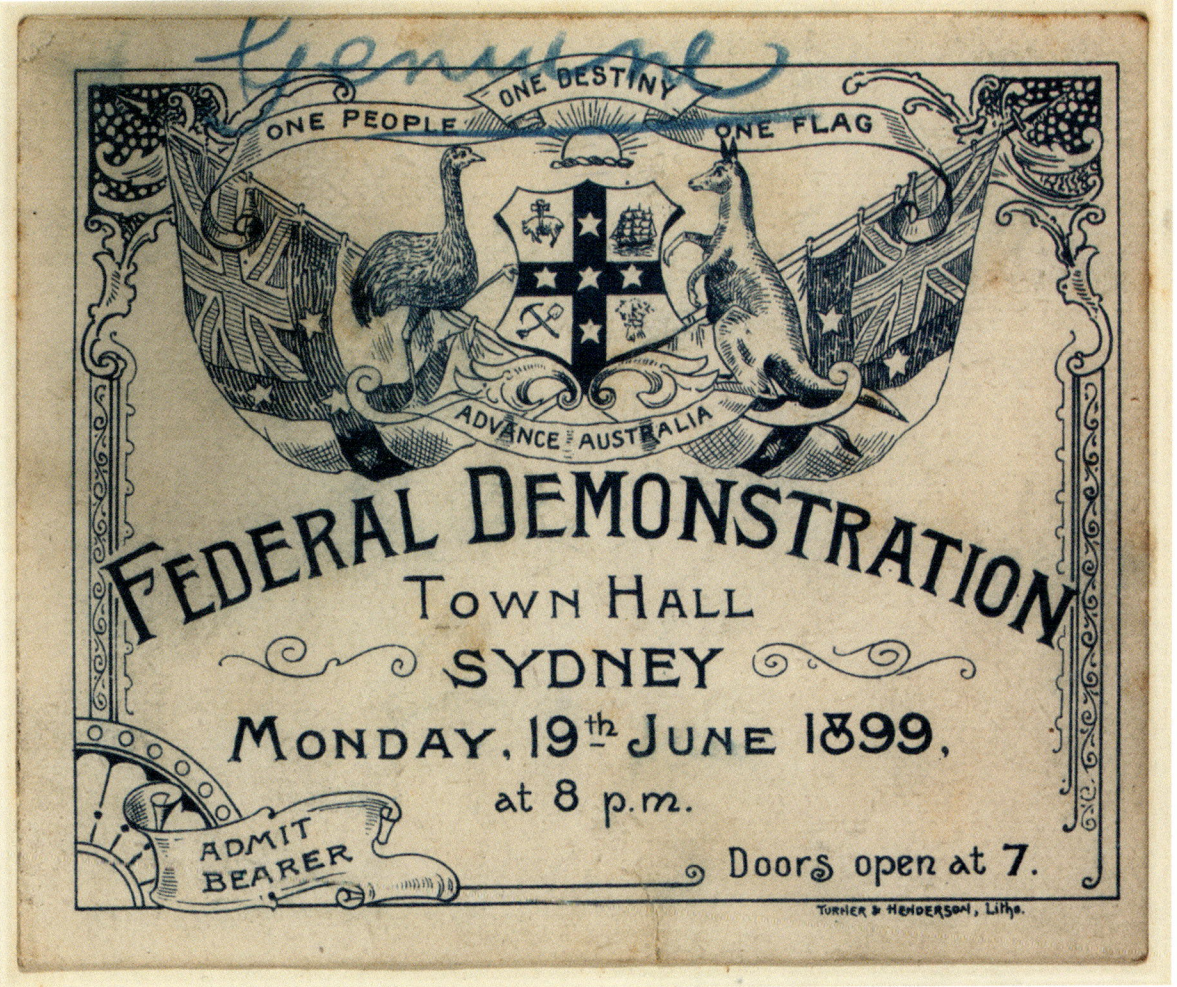

BELOW:

Nicholson and Bingle's Australian National Flag, 1823.
Based on a British naval ensign, this flag set the style for the Federation Flag first unfurled four decades later.

The flag was further debased several years later when some well-meaning, yet anonymous official, who, in wanting to symbolize the five existing Australian colonies, added a star to the centre of the St. George cross. This caused many to complain that so many stars smacked of too much American influence although this 'National Colonial Flag' was in reality a British White Ensign — with stars added — almost identical to the Australian federation flag which enjoyed enormous popularity before 1900.

After the first century of European settlement in Australia, several generations of Australians had been born and bred beneath the Southern Cross. The largest island in the world was split into six separate colonies, each with its own system of government, its own set of rules and its own separate relationship with the mother country. There were in these colonies distinctly recognizable patterns of migration, settlement and at times attitudes; Victoria had never been a penal colony, but both New South Wales and Tasmania were most certainly coloured with the 'convict stain', and the Vandemonian (Tasmanian) was the most despised of all.

The settlement of Queensland had a shaky start, taking years for Europeans to establish a

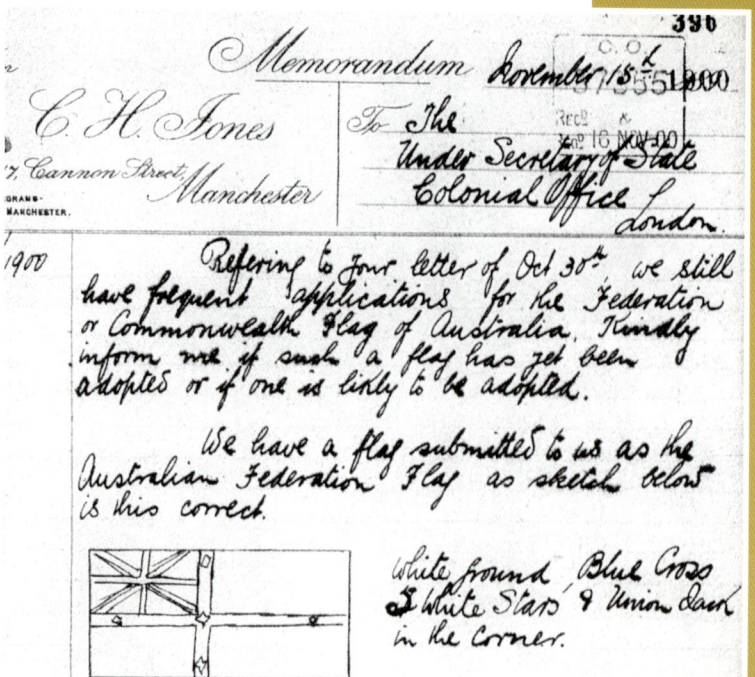

ABOVE:

Memo from [flag-maker] C.H. Jones to the Under-Secretary of State, Colonial Office London, 15 November 1900.

Mr. Jones was enquiring of the status of the Federation Flag, which had been in popular use since the early 1890s.

He thought that because of continued requests it was the design likely to be adopted by the newly federated nation.

(Courtesy Australian National Archives)

Terra Nullius

ABOVE:
The Federation Flag (1867).
Based on the British White Ensign with stars that reprise the design of the Eureka Flag of 1854, this Federation League flag was to be unfurled by Prince Alfred, Australia's first royal visitor, at a banquet in Melbourne in 1867.

Fearing for his safety the Prince disappointed the crowd of 60 000 high-spirited revellers and changed his itinerary — the royal personnage didn't show but the committee raised the flag anyway.

BELOW:
Souvenir federation pin, c. 1900.
(Courtesy National Library of Australia)

foothold in that harsh and challenging environment, but by the time journalist Andrew 'Banjo' Paterson penned 'Waltzing Matilda' in 1893, the curious song that quickly became the nation's unofficial anthem, Queensland had taken its place proudly alongside the older colonies and all of the colonies were ready for change.

Yet there were many who resisted the inevitable push towards merging of the colonies into one unified nation. Old jealousies, rivalries, pride and politicians often stood in the way of a smooth transition.

'We cannot stand that progressive colony, they are rather too insolent,' remarked Sir John Robinson, five-times Premier of New South Wales, who openly disliked Victoria. Although that colony in the south had only enjoyed half of the 19th century as an independent legislature, freed of rule from New South Wales in 1851, there were many prominent men in Victoria who were eager to realize the destiny of all Australia by bringing the fortunes of all the colonies together, sharing a common-wealth, through the federation of the states.

English writer Rudyard Kipling offered this advice when considering the lengthy deliberations over nationhood taken by the founding fathers prior to federation in 1901: 'If you want to hurry up federation, you ought to make a syndicate to hire a few German cruisers to bombard Sydney, Melbourne and Brisbane for twenty minutes. There'd be a federated Australia within twenty-four hours.'

A new nation, the Federation of Australian States, was brought into being on 1 January 1901, a revolutionary alignment of all peoples of the Australian continent — one people, one nation, one destiny — without bloodshed, not a shot fired, not a life lost, nor a sword drawn, although it did take a considerable effort to finally convince the west of the benefits of joining with the east.

The Australian federation was born of goodwill and ideals, not of avarice and greed, and not of despots nor dictators. The founding fathers shared a desire to bring together all of those things that bind Australians together beneath the Southern Cross.

We've the stars to show where we're going and the old flag to show where we've been.

– ROBIN NORTHOVER

ABOVE:
The Austral:'Umbrellas and Walking Sticks' available at Gowings, c.1911.

LEFT:
Sons of Britannia. A Federation Song.
The Federation Flag, shown on this song-sheet alongside the Union Jack and the Stars and Stripes, had long been recognized as the symbol of the federation movement, and most expected it to be the design adopted by the new nation.

The only problem was that the flag had been based on the early Australian Ensign (in those days the colony of New South Wales was Australia), and it was not all that long since several of the newer colonies had enjoyed separation from that jurisdiction.

It is no doubt that Victoria and Queensland were keen to have any flag other than one that looked like the old New South Wales flag.

(Bicentennial Copying Project, State Library of New South Wales)

Upon federation, a new nation demanded a new standard. The Melbourne newspaper, the *Review of Reviews* instigated a competition for a new flag for the new nation. Although there had been many attempts to design a new flag for Australia well before 1901, the political division between the colonies made acceptance impossible. The Federation

Terra Nullius

ABOVE:
Birth of the Commonwealth. Souvenir bookmark, 1901.

(Courtesy Mitchell Library, State Library of New South Wales)

ABOVE:
Invitation to Commonwealth Celebrations, Sydney, 2 January 1901.

The flag within the shield shows red-filled stars set on a striped background.

How did anyone ever make sense of all these images? No wonder Aussies are so ambivalent.

(Courtesy National Library of Australia)

Flag proposed by the Australian Federation League as far back as 1893, (based on the British naval ensign with the addition of the Southern Cross) remains one of the more attractive efforts. Most earlier designs reflect ancient heraldry, replete with arcane symbols bearing little relevance to Australian geography, and often failing to keep apace of modern movements in the visual arts and contemporary design.

The beginning of the 20th century saw exciting developments in technologies, in manufacturing, conceptual thinking and the arts. The 1900s ushered in the 'modern age', and any new design needed to look forward to complement this new modernism.

Before long the new federal government joined with the *Review of Reviews* and together they offered the prize of £150 for the best design for a new flag. A further £50 was donated by the Havelock Tobacco Company, to make a total prize pool of £200 (which was equivalent to at least four year's wages at the time).

One of the conditions of entry was that the design was to be based: 'on British Ensigns, as the flag of the country added to its folds, signalling to the beholder that it is an Imperial Union Ensign of the British Empire.'

This meant that the Union Flag of Britain was essential to any new design. As five of the judges were British naval officers who refused to countenance any design that didn't feature the Union Flag, its inclusion was mandatory. No matter whose creative minds went to work on the new flag, it was foreshadowed that the design should be based on the Red or Blue British ensigns. The Union flag was to be retained to indicate to the world that newly-

ABOVE:
'Young Australia' wrapped in the flag, 1921.
(Courtesy Australian Archives Collection. A1861, 4638)

OPPOSITE:
Invitation to the great Exhibition Buildings in Melbourne.
The temporary seat of the first Australian parliament for twenty years.
(Courtesy National Library of Australia)

federated Australia was still 'inferior' to Great Britain—make no mistake about that.

The competition, officially gazetted on 29 April 1901, and announced by the first Prime Minister of Australia, Edmund Barton, attracted 32 823 entries. Barton also announced the winner of the competition five months later at the Melbourne Exhibition Buildings, site of the first temporary Australian Parliament, on 3 September 1901. This report from the Melbourne *Age* newspaper of 4 September 1901, describes the result of the competition:

> At the Exhibition Building yesterday afternoon the Countess of Hopetoun opened the Commonwealth Flag and Seal Exhibition and announced the names of the successful competitors.
>
> The event was timed for 2.30pm and at that hour a large number of people had assembled about the entrances, attracted by the absolutely unique occasion. Among those present were a goodly sprinkling of legislators, both Federal and State, and a number of clergymen of various denominations.
>
> As Lady Hopetoun entered, a huge Blue Ensign with the prize design of the Southern Cross and a six-pointed star thereon was run up to the top of the flagstaff on the dome and breaking, streamed out on the heavy south-westerly breeze, a brave and inspiring picture.
>
> On entering the rooms reserved for the thousands of designs which go to make up the exhibition, the beholders were almost dazzled by the polychromatic spectacle which greeted their eyes. Every conceivable and inconceivable combination of colours flared from the walls which were spread from top to bottom with the artistic, inartistic and, in many instances, weird designs sent in, and for a few minutes the feeling was truly overpowering. After making a brief inspection of the principle designs which had been awarded prizes or honourable mention, Lady Hopetoun seated herself at the prize table.
>
> The Prime Minister rose and said that the Countess of Hopetoun had kindly consented to open the Exhibition, but before doing so wanted him to explain how the competition had come about and how it had resulted.

The Prime Minister read the following letter from the judges of the competition dated 2 September:

ABOVE:
Unity is Strength.
This souvenir handkerchief from 1900 leaves no doubt about the state of imperial power in a federated Australia.
(Courtesy National Library of Australia)

OPPOSITE:
Winning entries on display in the Exhibition Buildings in Melbourne.
From the *Review of Reviews*, 20 September 1901.
(Courtesy La Trobe Library, State Library of Victoria)

Sir,

Attracted by the loyalty and sentiment of the Australian people as represented by the 30,000 designs for a national flag, the great majority of which contain the Union Jack and the Southern Cross. It was felt that the only additional emblem was one representing the Federation of the 6 States. This was supplied by various forms such as coloured bars, shields, devices, stars, figures, letters, animals, etc. introduced in various forms, colours, positions on the various designs.

Having carefully examined every exhibit with due regard to history, heraldry, blazonry, distinctiveness, utility and cost of making it up in bunting, it was apparent that a Commonwealth Flag, to be representative, should contain:

1. The Union Jack on a blue or red ground;

2. A six-pointed star, representing the federated states of Australia, immediately underneath the Union Jack and pointing directly to the centre of St. George's Cross, in a size to occupy the major portion of one quarter of the Flag;

3. The Southern Cross; in the Fly, as indicative of the sentiment of the Australian nation.

Many designs were rejected as not being in accord with heraldry-borders around the Union Jack, contrary to the heraldry and blazonry of flags . . . crosses, coloured stars, stars too small to be seen at a distance, and otherwise faulty in design.

In conclusion we may state that our task was not an easy one, but our desire was to give the people of our new-born nation a symbol that would be endearing and lasting in its effect, and with that end in view we hope that we have been successful.

Five entrants had submitted almost identical designs and were to share equally in the honour of designing the new nation's own flag. Annie Dorrington, an artist from Perth; 14-year-old Ivor Evans of Melbourne, whose father was the flagmaker Evan Evans; 18-year-old Leslie John Hawkins, a teenager apprenticed to a Sydney optician; 35-year-old Prahran architect Egbert John Nuttall; and William Stevens, a ship's officer from Auckland, all received £40 each for their efforts.

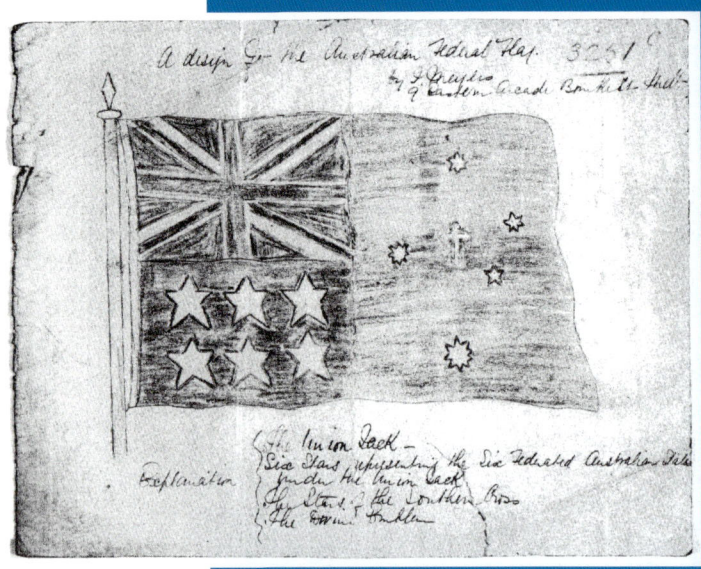

Above:

Design sketch submitted to the Review of Reviews.

The number of designs that were similar is not all that astonishing considering the parameters set by the judging panel.

This design by J. Meyers of Melbourne has all the elements: the Union Jack, with six stars representing the federated states below, the stars of the Southern Cross surrounding 'the divine emblem' (Christian cross) at the right.

This was not a flag for a future multi-cultural and secular nation.

(Courtesy Australian Archives Collection, A1719, 3251C)

Terra Nullius

The *Review of Reviews* has given the photograph shown at left the caption, 'Ivor Evans', as Ivor was only fourteen at the time, this is clearly not his portrait.

It is assumed that this is a portrait of his father, the flag-maker, Evan Evans.

ABOVE AND UPPER RIGHT:
The five winners of the Review of Reviews *flag design competition.*

Each of the five submitted almost identical designs and all were honoured. From the left: Annie Dorrington of Perth, Western Australia; E. J. Nutall of Prahran, Victoria; Ivor Evans of Melbourne, Victoria; 17 year-old L. J. Hawkins from Sydney, New South Wales and W. Stevens from New Zealand.

These portraits were published in the *Review of Reviews* 20 September 1901.

RIGHT:
One of the more interesting designs submitted for the competition.

Based on the Union Jack this design shows in the centre a map of Australia featuring the emu and kangaroo around the map are included the scottish thistle, the english rose, a bunch of shamrocks, and photographs of navy vessels.

(Courtesy La Trobe Library, State Library of Victoria)

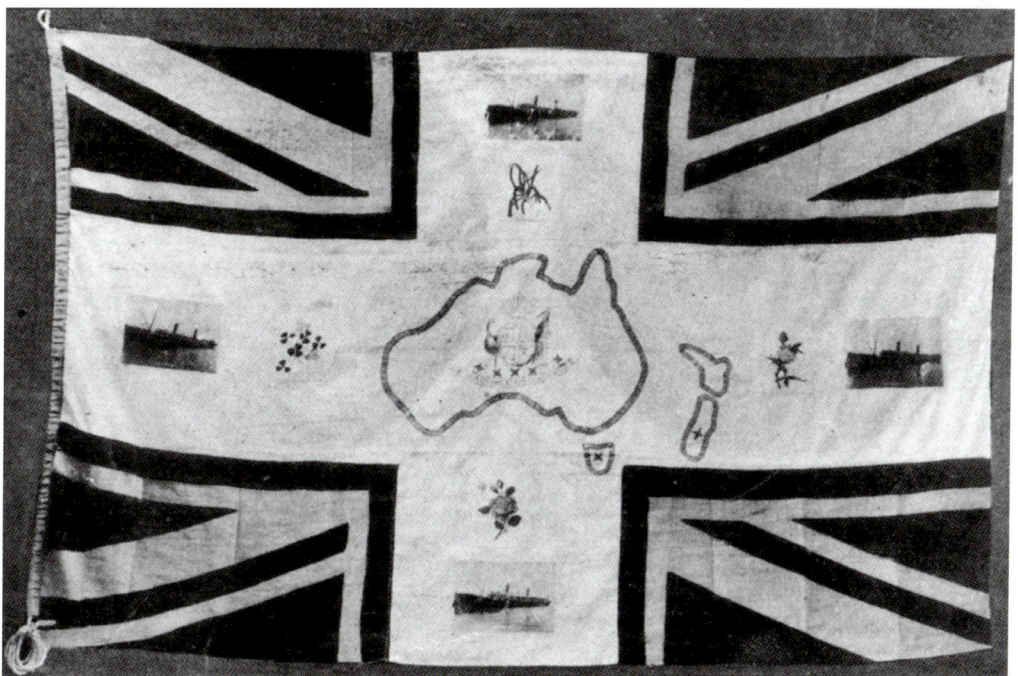

RIGHT:

Historical designs for the Australian Commonwealth Flag.

The design signed with the *nom de plume* of *Hec Clari Astris'* shows Lord Cecil and seven soldiers representing New Zealand and the six states of Australia.

At the time of Australia's federation there had been serious discussion about including New Zealand in the commonwealth, but in the end the 'kiwis' declined the offer to join with Australia. It's just as well really, or else the brave 'Anzacs' would only be known as the brave 'Aacs' today—and who would ever want to eat an Aac biscuit? (Australian Army Corps).

(Courtesy La Trobe Library, State Library of Victoria)

OPPOSITE:

Just a few of over 32 000 flag designs displayed in the Exhibition Building in Melbourne on 3 September 1901.
From the *Review of Reviews*, 20 September 1901.

(Courtesy La Trobe Library, State Library of Victoria)

The first design was almost identical to the design seen today except that the Federation Star had only six points and the stars of the Southern Cross had points ranging in number from five to nine, representing their apparent brightness in the sky. At the time the ensign in use had a field of red for civil use and blue for state's use only.

The adoption of the National Flag for Australia was never debated in the national parliament; the design was simply sent to the imperial authorities in England for approval. It was almost a year later when in late 1902 King Edward VII finally notified the Australian government that the flag had imperial approval. This was gazetted on 20 February 1903.

The flag has changed several times, the first in 1903 when, apparently to facilitate ease of manufacture, all but the smallest star of the Southern Cross were to be made with seven points. The second change was made after Australia had acquired the territory of Papua. The Federation Star was increased to seven points in recognition of this acquisition in 1908. Although the Northern Territory and the Australian Capital Territory were created in 1911, it was agreed that the seventh point on

the Federation Star would represent all territories created after 1901.

However, although the flag had imperial approval, it still had no legal status. It remained a national flag in intention only and could not be flown above the flag of Great Britain, but could only be flown inferior to, and in conjunction with, the British flag at all occasions.

LEFT:

Song sheets 1901.

There were many proposals for a new national anthem, and while many were published and enjoyed some degree of popularity 'God Save The King (Queen)' remained Australia's anthem for the next seventy years.

'Awake! Awake! Australia' was written by Scots-born Peter Dods McCormick, the composer of 'Advance Australia Fair'.

'Advance Australia Fair' was first performed at a St. Andrew's Day ceremony in Sydney in 1878.

It was the then Labor leader, Arthur Caldwell, who many years later convinced the Australian Broadcasting Commission to play the tune ahead of the news, and it was so widely recognized that almost 100 years after its first performance it finally gained acceptance as the unofficial national anthem.

Both song sheets have embraced the early designs of the flag which were readily bound into the Australian symbolic lexicon.

(Far left: Courtesy Australian Archives, A1786, 8281B)
(Left: Courtesy Mitchell Library, State Library of New South Wales)

OPPOSITE:

Flying the flag on the Australia Building, London, 1901.

The flag flying from the mast simply states 'Australia'; the smaller flags are flags bearing states emblems on British ensigns.

(Photograph by H.W. Mosby, courtesy Alfred Deakin Collection, National Library of Australia)

Curiously enough, it was the then Prime Minister of Australia, Robert Menzies, a staunch patriot, monarchist and anglophile, whose government passed the *Flags Act (1953)* which ushered in a new era for Australia's sense of its own sovereignty. This act required the Australian flag be flown superior to all others, including even the British flag. The *Flags Act* also technically changed the flag again, as it declared the Blue Ensign was to be the national and military flag and the red to be the state and civil ensign. The blue 'Southern Cross' was to be, for the first time, the official, Australian National Flag.

This act was given assent by Queen Elizabeth II on her first visit to Australia on 15 April 1954,

The Australian Flag ~ The First 100 Years

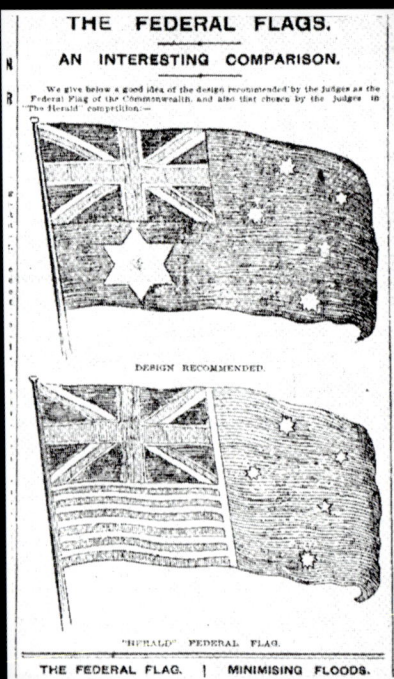

Above:
Early designs for the Australian flag.
A pattern was surely emerging amongst the aspiring designers.

Above and Left:
The Melbourne *Herald* didn't like the chosen design at all and ran a disgruntled campaign against it.

The first of the three designs shown at left were chosen by the *Herald* as their preferred winner; they obviously felt that a little bit of 'Americana' could go a long way.

Thank heavens no-one was listening.

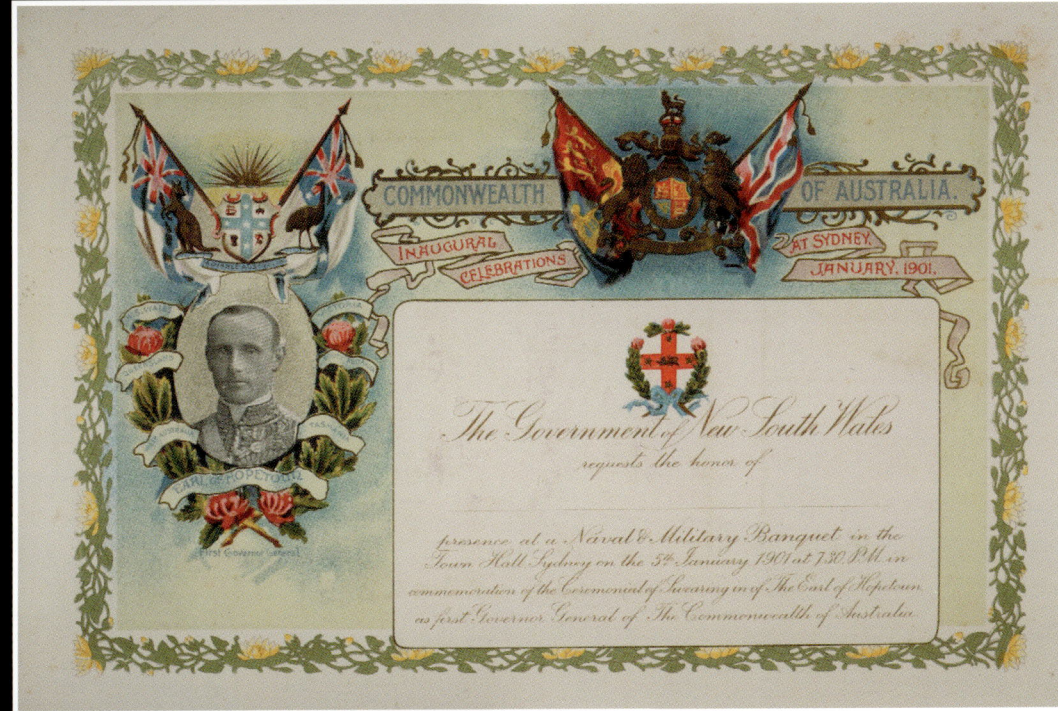

ABOVE:
Invitation to a military banquet in New South Wales.

The invitation shows any number of national emblems, flags and flora and fauna.

This ambivalence to symbology has persisted for over a century.

(Courtesy Mitchell Library, State Library of New South Wales)

BELOW:
Kangaroo Flag designs shown in the Review of Reviews, *20 September 1901.*

(Courtesy La Trobe Library, State Library of Victoria)

also making this the first act of an Australian parliament that had received assent from the monarch rather than the viceroy. It is also curious that the British monarch was eager to take the first step on the journey which may lead eventually to Australia's complete independence from Britain.

After 53 years the flag was at last able to be hoisted above all others and declare Australia's sovereignty. As the slogan of the Australian Federation League had extolled when it was formed in 1893 ('One People ... One Destiny ... One Flag'), the Southern Cross was at last the official symbol of that one nation.

December 1st 1854

Swearing allegiance to the "Southern Cross"

Above
Digger's' leader, Peter Lalor.

Opposite:
Swearing Allegiance to the 'Southern Cross'. 1 December 1854.
Watercolour by Charles Doudiet.

(Courtesy Ballarat Fine Art Gallery)

WHOSE COUNTRY? WHICH FLAG?

Long before Australia was a federated nation with its own flag, several historical incidents revealed the desire of colonial Australians to band together under a flag they identified as their own, and clearly distinct from that of other nations. In many ways, these incidents, which more often than not took place on the colonial goldfields some 150 years ago, are paralleled by similar historical events today as many Australians push to free the Australian National Flag of the Union Jack. The incident at Eureka on the Ballarat goldfields in 1854 is perhaps one of the most notable early events.

On 1 December of that year, a large group of diggers on the Eureka lead gathered together beneath a new standard fluttering on a pole set in a clearing in the bush. They were protesting against the corruption of the goldfields officials, a despotic governor, and the universally hated gold licence fee.

They banded together in protest to swear allegiance to their flag, the Southern Cross, and declared: 'We swear by the Southern Cross to truly stand by each other, and defend our rights and liberties'. This was to become known as the 'Diggers Oath' and it ushered in a great change on the Australian political scene.

The flag was made of bright blue and emblazoned with a white cross. In each corner of the cross and at its centre were sewn five large eight-pointed stars. Most believe that the blue represented the sky and the stars of the constellation upon it; others believe the blue represented the diggers, as most wore blue shirts at that time.

It may simply have been a choice made for convenience, or perhaps the colour was chosen to differentiate the Eureka movement from the 'Red-Ribbon Rebellion', an earlier protest against the gold licence fee where, on 27 August 1853, diggers took to wearing red ribbons after a great meeting was held at View Point on the Bendigo diggings. The red-ribbon agitation, as it was known, did make a design decision of convenience: Red was the colour of the undershirts commonly worn by the diggers, a cloth easy to source on the diggings before, and very difficult after, the rebellion.

At an even earlier meeting on the Forest Creek diggings (Mt. Alexander), on 15 December 1851, over 14 000 diggers joined in protest at the government's management of the diggings and the cost of the monthly licence to dig for gold. They rallied beneath the 'Diggers Flag'.

It is difficult to read the only drawings available of this event but a description of a similar flag, painted two years later by a Mr. Dexter for the View Point (Red Ribbon) Rebellion, is well documented.

In Bendigo, traveller and journalist, William Howitt, followed behind a large procession where the revolutionary flags of France and Germany, the Stars and Stripes of America, the Union Jack of the United Kingdom, and a long green banner held aloft by the Irish and finally the Diggers Flag all came together in one colourful protest. Howitt recorded that the Diggers Flag: 'showed the pick, the shovel, and the cradle; that represented labour. There were the scales; that meant justice. There was the Roman bundle of sticks; that meant union: altogether; all up at once. There were the kangaroo and emu; that meant Australia.'

It is clear that the flag, as a symbol, has always been recognized as one of the most important tools for bringing together peoples of like minds, or peoples of common experience. The flags were one of the first products of these protests, a rallying point, an identifiable symbol of the aspirations of each and every one of those disaffected diggers who stood beneath it.

There were those in government who dismissed the protesters as revolutionists, foreigners, chartists and worst of all, democrats. Yet in Bendigo, the British would hear no seditious remarks against their beloved Queen. In the midst of the agitation the Union Jack was raised high into the air, the Britons insisted on their patriotism to 'Queen and Country' while protesting about the iniquities of her law-makers.

There were those who dimissed the agitators at Ballarat as a purely Irish business, yet there were many who also had experience of British Rule and British interference in the affairs of

ABOVE:
The great meeting of diggers at the old shepherd's hut, Forest Creek diggings, 15 December 1851.
Engraving by Thomas Ham, Melbourne 1852.
(Courtesy Queen Victoria Museum Launceston)

OPPOSITE PAGE:
The Diggers' Flag, 1853.
Based on the description by William Howitt, an eye-witness to the 'red ribbon' protest meeting in Bendigo in August 1853.
(Interpretation by Rhyll Plant)

Whose Country? Which Flag?

Masthead of the Gold Diggers' Advocate, *22 July 1854.*

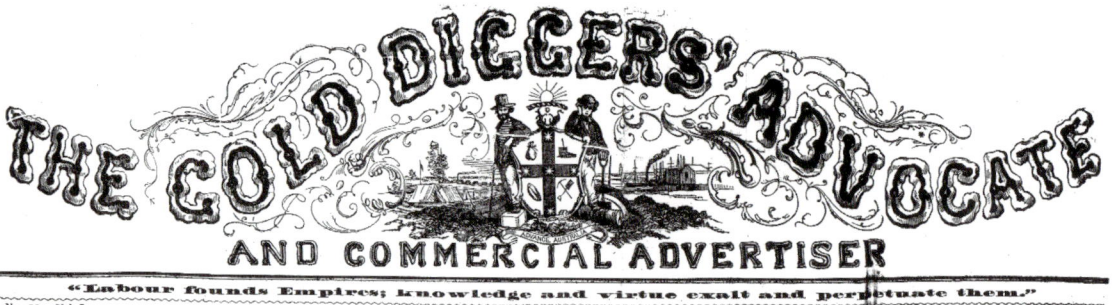

ABOVE:

Crest on the Ballarat Mining Exchange. This symbolic crest is similar to the design of the masthead of the *Gold Diggers' Advocate*, a newspaper that was strongly supportive of the Eureka miners.

Published in Melbourne by chartist George Black and diggers leader Henry Holyoake, the *Advocate* showed in its crest the pick and shovel, kangaroo and emu, scales of justice and money bag.

The Diggers Flag carried at Bendigo was almost identical. The main difference was the money bag; it had replaced the bundle of sticks.

It appears even then this newspaper recognized that individual pursuits would eventually override collective strength as a motivating force in the young society growing out of the goldfields.

(Photograph courtesy the Author)

their homelands. The Americans, Canadians, French, Germans and Italians, of whom there were many, were only too ready to line up against the troopers and claim independence in this new land beneath the Southern Cross.

It was at Ballarat that saw the ultimate showdown between the diggers and the government. On 1 December 1854 the Southern Cross (Eurka) Flag was raised over the crude stockade that the diggers had built at Eureka, where they drilled and marched backwards and forwards in an attempt to achieve some sort of preparedness for their inevitable battle with the forces of the government.

Little did they expect the tragedy which would unfold when the troopers of the 40th Regiment mounted a surprise attack on their stockade at dawn on Sunday morning, 3 December 1854. Most of the diggers were still in their beds sleeping off their Saturday night's revelry when the crackle of rifle fire rang out across the valley.

A bloody battle raged for only a short while, and as the dust settled and the gunsmoke drifted away 22 diggers and six troopers lay dead or dying. Trooper John King clambered up the bush pole in the centre of the clearing and ripped the 'Southern Cross' from its crude halyard. He trampled the diggers' standard into the dust and pierced it several times with his bayonet. King kept the flag as a souvenir of the diggers' defeat at the Eureka Stockade.

Almost half a century later his widow gave the flag to the Ballarat Fine Art Gallery for safekeeping, with the added proviso that the flag was on loan only and not a gift to the gallery. The ownership of the Eureka Flag remained a bone of contention that continued to fuel

RIGHT:

The Eureka Flag.

It is generally agreed that the Eureka Flag was designed by a Canadian digger 'Lieutenant' Ross and made by the wives of two diggers who were also on the Eureka diggings.

Others have laid claim to the design; one John W. Wilson wrote in 1885 that he had had a flag of the same design made by a tentmaker and had placed it in his own tent for safekeeping the night before the battle.

But when the troopers attacked the diggers encampment in the early dawn of 3 December 1854, Ross had his flag already flying from a tall tree cut from nearby Byles Swamp and erected in the centre of the stockade. Ross died defending this flag.

It appears that Wilson's may have been one of several flags made of the same design but it is Ross's that was torn from its pole by Trooper John King and dragged through the dust after the battle of Sunday morn.

It is this (Ross's) flag that hangs today in the Ballarat Art Gallery, and which has been the subject of ownership debate for the past 150 years.

(Courtesy Ballarat Fine Art Gallery)

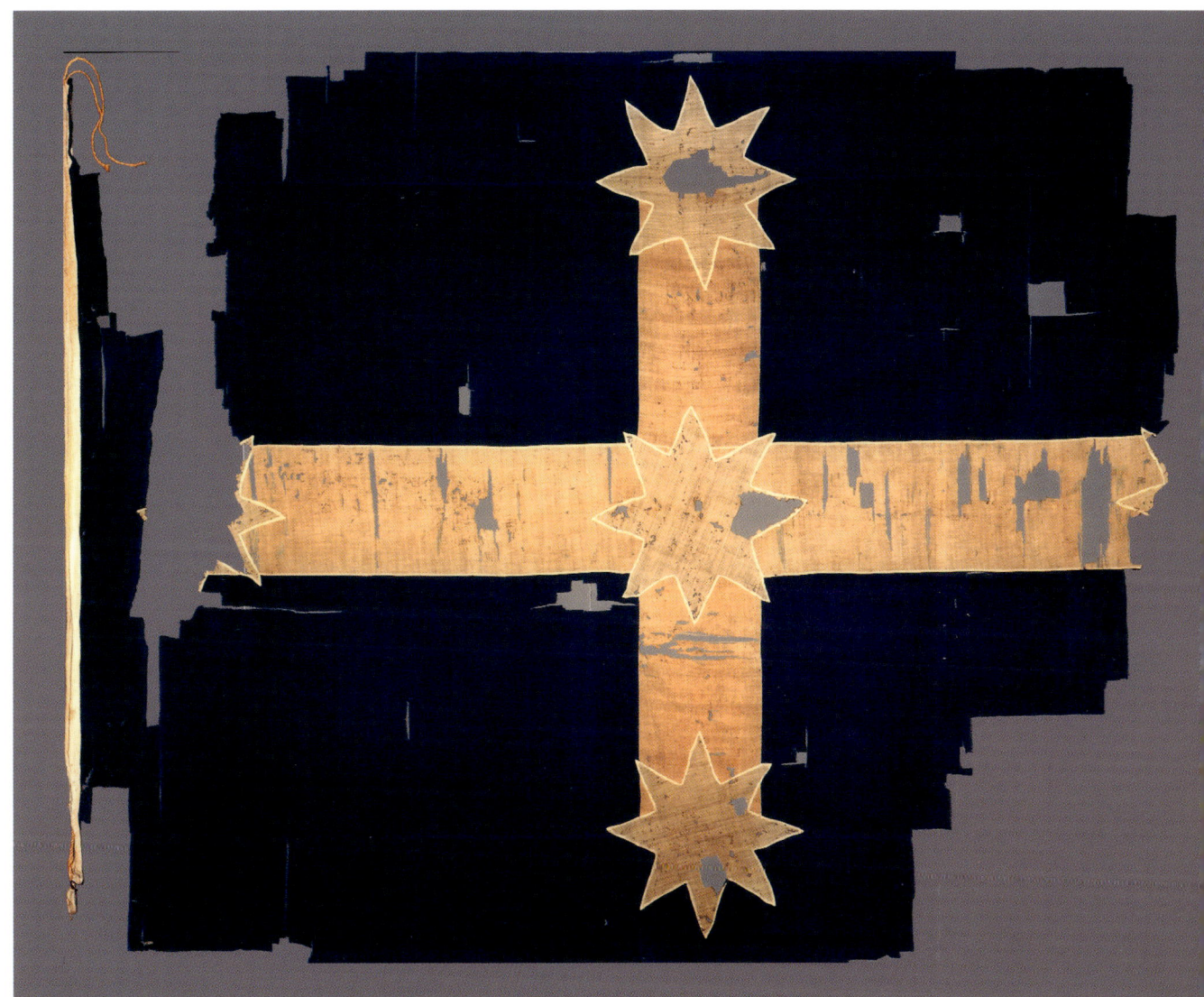

debate in Ballarat for nearly 150 years. Descendants of the Eureka 'rebels' claimed the flag as their own property; the Ballarat Fine Art Gallery claimed it as its own, and a letter from Mrs. King to the gallery written on 1 October 1895 (which only surfaced in October 2000) states that it remains the property of John King's descendants.

Victoria Police-Sergeant Peter Lalor, the great-grandson of the digger's leader of the same name, Peter Lalor, and Paul Murphy, whose great-grandfather was also at the stockade, laid claim to ownership of the flag. Their claim states that the flag was the property of the Ballarat Reform League, and that although the flag was captured after the battle, and that all of those within the stockade where charged with treason, none were convicted of that or any other charge. Therefore, the flag which was held as Crown evidence should have been returned to its owners or creators as it was no longer the subject of any proven criminal act.

Lalor and Murphy hoped to install the original Eureka Flag in the newly created Museum and Interpretation Centre which has been built on the site of the original stockade, on the other side of Ballarat to the gallery. To add insult to their injury, the gallery stands on roughly the position that the troopers were camped just before the attack on 3 December; to them this means that their flag is, today, held in 'enemy territory'.

Marilyn Rich, the Director of the Ballarat Art Gallery, publicly stated that the flag would only be removed from the gallery 'over [her] dead body', which should make for an interesting debate in years to come in that solid central Victorian city.

LEFT:

Page 2 of a letter from F.J. Riley to his father after a visit to Ballarat Art Gallery in 1912.

The letter included a portion of the flag that had been snipped off by the caretaker and given to Riley as a memento of his visit.

He wrote: 'strange to say no one there seems to value it [the Eureka Flag] in the least, it is hung over a trestle affair — fully exposed to the public — well I got into a conversation with the keeper or the caretaker of the Gallery and persuaded him to give me a bit of the flag, and much to my surprise and astonishment he gave me a bit. I was with him when he tore it off.

It seems wanton sacrilege, vandalism or something worse to tear it — still he did ...'.

(Courtesy National Library of Australia)

OPPOSITE:

The Eureka Stockade Centre, Ballarat.

This huge flag flies prominently over the exact spot on which the battle of 3 December took place.

The Eureka Stockade Museum and Interpretation centre at Ballarat has an excellent collection and display telling the story of the events that led up to the battle.

It has everything — but the flag.

(Photograph courtesy the Author)

The matter of ownership of the original Eureka Flag was resolved — for the moment at least — in late 2001 when Trooper King's descendants finally handed over ownership to the Ballarat Fine Art Gallery.

The debate over the Eureka Flag continues to capture the imagination, in particular, of those contemporary Australians committed to the republican movement. There are many in Australian society who believe that the 'Eureka' Southern Cross is the only flag for an Australian republic, but there are just as many who believe the opposite. Whatever the resolution of this long debate one thing seems certain: the stars of the Southern Cross will be somewhere in evidence; the future of the design in the upper left corner is, however, less certain.

In his film *Reckless Kelly*, Australian actor, director, comedian and contemporary larrikin Yahoo Serious makes a strong point in favour of a new Australian flag when he confronts an incorrigible businessman Sir John, played by Hugo Weaving, in his office suite high above Sydney's streets. Sir John is plotting to deprive the Kelly gang of its 'spiritual' home, Reckless Island, by severing it from its foundations and transporting it to Japan. Serious, in the role of young Ned Kelly, bursts into his office and slices the Union Jack from an Australian flag hanging behind Sir John's des. Kelly then pins a cloth upon which a kangaroo is printed to the wall in the place where the British flag once hung. It turns out that the kangaroo is cut from a bar towel from Kelly's

LEFT:
Anti-Chinese Flag, Lambing Flat.
Another Southern Cross flag was flown by the diggers on the Lambing Flat goldfields near Young in central New South Wales on 30 June 1861—only this time the diggers weren't protesting for democratic reform, just the opposite: they were protesting about the number of Chinese miners on the field.

Lambing Flat was a pretty rough goldfield and had attracted some famous and some unsavoury characters to this remote diggings, well away from the easy reach of the law. Among them were Ben Hall, Frank 'Darkie' Gardiner, Johnny Gilbert, John Dunne and the Clarke Brothers.

It was these likely lads and hundreds of others who marched, 'liquored up', behind a large tent-fly painted with the words 'Roll Up, Roll Up, No Chinese' and with a white-starred cross set against a brilliant blue ground.

The diggers drove the Chinese out of the valley, killing, looting and destroying as they went.

It is said that this incident laid the foundation of the 'White Australia Policy' which took almost a further 100 years to be abolished.

Such outlaws had disgraced the nascent emblem of Australian pride. It also took almost 100 years for the Southern Cross to fly freely again—to take its place as a symbol of Australian independence, not one born of bigotry.

(Courtesy Young Historical Museum)

Whose Country? Which Flag?

ABOVE:
Sturt Street Ballarat.
The Southern Cross remains a powerful image in the central Victorian City of Ballarat. The city uses the flag as its own corporate symbol and many businesses have also appropriated the name and design.

1. *Ausflag* is a Sydney based-organization established in 1981 dedicated to the promotion of a truly Australian flag.

RIGHT:
Reconciliation Flag, 1999.
This flag has been adopted by the Australian indigenous people as a banner of reconciliation.

Pub, the Glenrowan Hotel, and the subsequent seizure of Reckless Island is a response to some quick forensic work by Sir John on the towel.

At the point when Kelly cuts the Union Jack from the wall and the kangaroo is pinned in its place, a cry of recognition and then delight ripples through an Australian audience. Although many Australians don't see the need to change the flag, most take delight in the symbolism.

The real Ned Kelly (1855–80) offered a similar opinion over a century earlier than his celluloid namesake in his 7500-word long 'Jerilderie letter': 'What would England do if America declared war and hoisted a green flag, as its all Irishmen that has got command of her armies forts and batteries, even her very life guards and beef tasters are Irish, would they not slew around and fight her with their own arms for the sake of the colour they dare not wear ...'

On Australia Day 1998, the Melbourne *Age* and *Sydney Morning Herald* newspapers published 100 designs in a quest for a consensual opinion on a design for a new flag. Readers were asked to vote via Ausflag's[1] website for the design thought best to represent and unite the nation. The flags on the bottom row (see

page 54) were winners from previous attempts at finding a new flag for the nation.

On thing is certain, however: the stars of the Southern Cross and the old 'red, white and blue' continue to be popular in most designs. The kangaroo rated only an occasional mention and the green and gold even less, yet in the results of the poll the people's choice selected a design featuring the kangaroo both first and third, with second place being awarded to a design closely related to the Aboriginal flag.

Surprisingly, in a nation obsessed with sport, Aussies were ready to separate sporting symbolism from nationhood. The nation's sporting colours were seen for what they are, while the colours of the nation were a different matter altogether.

The 'Reconciliation Flag' (shown above) was created in 1999 by Melbourne-based designer and University lecturer Russell Kennedy.

The Australian Flag ~ The First 100 Years

LEFT:
Cathy Arnott with the Reconciliation Flag at Colonial Stadium, Melbourne.

'Flags are powerful representations of a country's image, integrity and security. The current flag debate is dominated by politics, tradition, race, sentiment and guilt, and Australians are not ready to agree on the issue.

'Flag loyalists argue that the Union Jack should be retained as the symbol of our origin, which is an insult to Aboriginal Australia.' — Russell Kennedy, designer.

The Aboriginal Flag designed by Harold Thomas in 1971 has been accepted as a legitimate symbol of Australia's indigenous peoples for many years.

Since the 1967 referendum, in which Australians voted overwhelmingly to recognize indigenous Australians, to count them on the national census and grant them franchise, the movement for full reconciliation has been gathering momentum.

The Reconciliation Flag attempts to combine the colours of the Aboriginal flag with a vision for a new, truly, Australian symbol.

ABOVE:
Bulletin *cover, 26 January 1963.*
Published to commemorate the 175th anniversary of the British landing at Sydney Cove, this drawing by the late Les Tanner shows Kennedy's United States of America, MacMillan's Britain and Sukarno's Indonesia all squabbling over the sovereignty of Australia.
(Courtesy News Limited)

Reconciliation Badge, 2000.

The idea of his reconciliation flag took several years to consolidate. Kennedy won the *Herald Sun*'s Flag Search Competition in 1993 with a similar design he called the 'Advance Australia' national flag.

He had shown his original design to Lois O'Donoghue, chairperson of the Aboriginal and Torres Strait Islands Commission's (ATSIC), a year earlier. She agreed with the general concept, but thought the colours of Kennedy's original design — a white Southern Cross with a blue kangaroo on a red background — may have reflected Australia's British heritage, but it did not represent Australia's first inhabitants.

On this advice Kennedy incorporated the colours from the current Aboriginal flag into this striking design creating a black kangaroo against the red-earth background and a yellow Southern Cross. The movement for a reconciliation flag has since gained momentum; a copy of the flag was given to every secondary school in Victoria in 2000, the Nillimbik Shire Council in Victoria officially recognized the flag, and it is also accepted by Aboriginal communities and indigenous organisations.

A century earlier the idea of 'our own flag for Australia' inspired the popular Australian poet and author Andrew 'Banjo' Paterson to add his voice to the debate at the end of the nineteenth century, with a sentiment that still echoes true today:

They mustered us with a royal din,
In wearisome weeks of drought,
Ere ever the half of the crops were in,
Or half of the sheds cut out.
'Twas down with saddle and spurs and whip,
The swagman dropped his swag,
And we hurried us off to an outbound ship,
To fight for the English flag,
The English flag . . . it is ours in sooth,
We stand by it wrong or right,
But deep in our hearts is the honest truth,
We fought for the sake of a fight.
And the English flag may flutter and wave,
Where the world-wide oceans toss,
But the flag the Australian dies to save,
Is the flag of the Southern Cross.

The Australian Flag ~ The First 100 Years

People's Choice No. 1.
Designed by George Margaritis, Victoria.

People's Choice No. 2.
Designed by Neville Cowland
and Judith North, Werribee, Victoria.

People's Choice No. 3.
Designed by Ausflag's Harold Scruby.

FAR LEFT:
A New Flag?

In the continued quest for a new Australian symbol the Melbourne *Age* newspaper published on Australia Day 1998 these 100 designs chosen from more than 2500 by Ausflag.

Aspects of the Aboriginal flag have heavily influenced many of the designs shown, where the colours red and black appear with regularity.

However, it appears that blue does dominate, and often in combination with orange.

Are Australians seeing a new symbolism emerging in these colours, the colours of the earth and the clear blue southern skies?

These are unique colours. They are colours that speak of Australia's place in the world.

They are not the colours of traditional heraldry, nor the symbols of old enmities or old conquests, but the colours of a new spirit. A spirit born of place, of environment and of a people freed from the past.

Are they the colours of the new Australia?

(Courtesy the Melbourne *Age* newspaper and Ausflag)

The judge's choice.

The judges of the 1998 flag competition run by the Melbourne *Age* and *Sydney Morning Herald* newspapers selected the three designs shown below as the winners.

ABOVE:

Cartoon by Ron Tanberg, published in the *Sydney Morning Herald*, 19 October 1996

(Courtesy Ron Tanberg and the *Sydney Morning Herald*)

First Prize.
Designed by Frank Gentil, Lewisham, New South Wales.

Second Prize.
Designed by George Margaritis, Richmond, Victoria.

Trademark: Southern Cross, manufacturers of roof cooling materials, c. 1899.

The Southern Cross has been a popular symbol of Australian aspiration, both commercial and spiritual, for well over a century — from Eureka to 'Reconciliation'.

Third Prize.
Designed by Peter Lambert, Ballarat, Victoria.

The Australian Flag ~ The First 100 Years

LEFT:
Troops from the 8th Contingent say farewell as they head off to war.
(Courtesy La Trobe Library, State Library of Victoria)

Above:
Australia Today cover, 1917.
Illustration by Norman Lindsay.

This cover shows diggers at the front with the spirit of Australia holding aloft the Red Ensign.

RALLY BEHIND... WHICH FLAG?

ABOVE:
Flag commemorating the Jubilee of Queen Victoria's reign, 1907.
A veteran of the Sudan and Boer wars, Tom Gunning decorated the flag with the names of all the battles in which he had fought.
(Courtesy Australian War Memorial)

CENTRE:
A soldier of the 2nd Australian Imperial Force (A.I.F.) shows the official Australian (Union Jack) flag on the way to battle, World War II.
(Courtesy La Trobe Library, State Library of Victoria)

Another flag debate continues to rage over which flag 'our boys fought and died under', and continues to divide opinion in Australia.

Whenever the suggestion is made to retire the flag from active service and replace it with a new design which meets the needs and desires of 21st-century Australians, it is met with howls of derision, anger and disgust.

Before long, a representative of the Returned Services League (RSL) is approached by the 'investigative' media and asked the same old question 'Should we change the flag?', and the same old answer is cranked out: 'You can't change the flag; it is disrespectful to all the diggers who fought, died and sacrificed their lives under it'.

Australians have fought under several flags during both World Wars. They rallied behind the Union Jack, the Red Ensign and the Blue Ensign.

While the Union Jack was certainly the honoured flag of Empire, the Aussies showed little respect for their English 'superior' officers. However the Australian digger had a great patriotism to 'King and Country'; even though that King lived in another country altogether.

The diggers would have remained faithful to their schoolyard lessons as they 'honoured the flag, served their King' and, no doubt, 'cheerfully obeyed their parents, teachers and the law'.

Australian soldiers went to war for the British empire in 1914 behind the Union Jack. Later, in 1939 it was Australian Prime Minister R.G. Menzies who responded immediately to Britain's declaration of war against Germany by announcing that as Britain was at war, so too, was Australia. Once again the Aussies went into battle to defend the British empire, with the flags of the empire flying before them, and the 'Southern Cross' in their knapsacks.

LEFT:

Frontispiece of The Anzac Book.

This curious illustration shows two flags, held aloft by both Aussie and Kiwi alike, with the seemingly calm waters of the Dardenelles behind.

The flags look curiously like angels wings shielding the 'Anzacs', but it is the centrally placed British Flag that binds the concept together as they are: 'worthy sons of Empire'.

(Courtesy A.K. Macdougall)

ABOVE:

The Union Jack bearing the signatures of members of the 2/21st Battalion, 23rd Brigade, 8 Division, 2nd A.I.F, with their colour patch in the centre, c. 1940.

(Courtesy Australian War Memorial)

OPPOSITE:

Australian field hospital decorated with the flags of the British Empire during the Boer War, 1899-1902.

(Courtesy National Library of Australia)

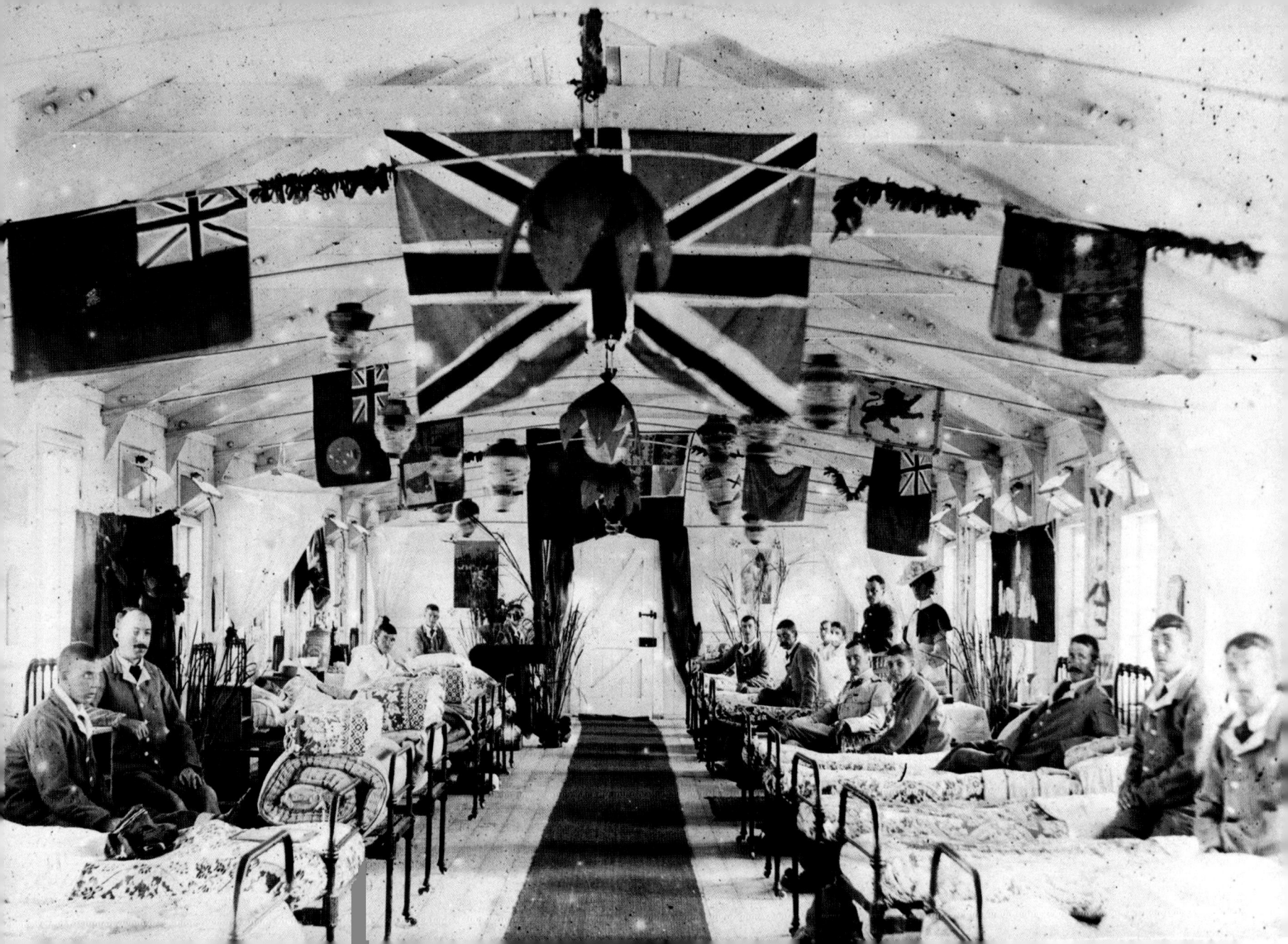

LEFT:

Commemorative poster from World War I.

The poster shows the badges and insignia worn by the Australian troops.

(Private Collection)

ABOVE:

Postcard from 'somewhere in France', World War I.

Many commentators on the conservative side of the flag debate make the common mistake in claiming that the Aussies fought under the modern version (Blue Ensign) of the National Flag of Australia — in both world wars.

In fact, the Union Jack was the flag of the British empire and took precedence over the Aussie flag. The blue flag was rarely seen other than in administrative (government) documents and on ceremonial occasions.

(Author's collection)

OPPOSITE:

A recruiting officer visits Jerseyville, New South Wales.

Volunteers, relatives and friends pose proudly in front of the Union Jack, c. 1914. How many would never see Jerseyville again?

(Bicentennial Copying Project. Courtesy State Library of New South Wales Collection)

Rally Behind...Which Flag?

The Australian Flag ~ The First 100 Years

Above:

A digger on leave, Charlie Bridge, would lay his flag on the footpath while young Irma recited poems such as 'It's only an old bit of bunting', etc.

Money was thrown on the flag and collected for the World War I charity 'Every Tommy's Sister-circle of war workers'.

(Bicentennial Copying Project. Courtesy State Library of New South Wales)

Above:

War Bonds poster World War I.

(Courtesy Australian War Memorial. AWM V5621)

Collecting for the cause!

Above:

War Bonds poster World War I.

(Courtesy National Library of Australia)

Souvenir from Egypt, 1915.

The souvenir trade boomed wherever the troops were stationed during World War I.

There was such a demand for items such as this silk embroidery and for embroidered postcards, that the Singer Sewing Machine Co. enjoyed an export boom for as long as the hostilities lasted and the Aussie boys wanted to send something home to mum.

This embroidery shows the Union Jack, and the French, Belgian and Australian Flags. Here the stars are shown white — pity the poor New Zealanders if this was a standard design.

(Author's collection)

men living this season may truly repeat to one another, "Mine eyes have seen the glory of the coming of the Lord."

A Bloodless Revolution

Sons of capitalists giving willing obedience to the military orders of wage earners in France who were their superior officers in the army, and wage-earning private soldiers rendering equal obedience to officer-capitalists; wives and daughters of wealth-performing works of mercy in sisterhood with proletrait women, nor asking the social status and banking references of those stricken ones to whom they ministered, did not dream that they were fomenting revolution at home. But they were. The revolution has taken visible form, and it is bloodless, except that labor's blood gushes hot in response to a new warmth of feeling manifested by capital toward labor. This feeling is manifested in public speeches and writings by individual capitalists, and finally it has taken answerable form in the resolutions adopted by your great organisation of industrial captains, the Chamber of Commerce of the State of New York.

The Federation of Labor of New York State hastens, through its duly authorised President, to make answer.

Chamber takes this viewpoint, and on its part expresses the belief that employers are no longer to be regarded as granite images, but as human beings like ourselves, animated by the same human impulses, with hearts like ours, affections like ours, endowed to the same fundamental right to life, liberty and the pursuit of happiness that we acknowledge as the common heritage of all men.

Seventh, that the Chamber makes reference to the efforts of "revolutionary or anarchistic bodies to make capital out of labor disputes." The Federation respectfully calls the Chamber's attention to the revolutionary, anarchistic, and inflammatory remarks of the president of a large national association of employers, recently uttered, which caused grave unrest in wage-earner circles as to the intentions of capital. The Federation advises the Chamber that no Syndicalists or I.W.W's are identified with organised labor.

Eighth, that "debate, discussion and compromise . . . has adjusted the disputes . . . in a manner which is orderly, reasonable, just, and in the end satisfactory." There can be no divergence between the Chamber and the Federation on this splendid pronouncement. Debate, discussion, com-

How can Labor and Capital be helpful to each other? The advisability of calling on all organisations and associations interested in the general Capital-Labor subject to select delegates to a State-wide meeting, where the perplexities of both employers and wage-earners may be fully considered, with the purpose of devising a plan for overcoming the difficulties which beset the industry.

The Federation has no formulated solution to propose, but its belief is strong that the collective wisdom of delegates to a State-wide joint session of Capital and Labor could not fail to produce beneficial results in the form of an agreement on united action.

£440 IN BANK NOTES BURNED

AUCKLAND, Tuesday.

A sum of £440 in bank notes was destroyed in an outbreak of fire in a farm house at Te Awamutu.

Such of the cable news on this page as is so headed has appeared in "The Times," and is cabled to "The Herald" by special permission. It should be understood that the opinions are not those of "The Times" unless expressly stated to be so.

ly, the gates being a little later than originally fixed. It is uncertain when the returning warships will leave Port Darwin.

AUCTIONEERS' NOTICES
SEE BACK PAGE

Messrs E. J. and H. Ames, Messrs Packer Bros.—Shop and villa sites at Carnegie, Murrumbeena, Glenhuntly, East Malvern, and Ormond, May 30, at 2.30 p.m.
Messrs Duncan and Weller—Subdivisional sale of Blanche estate, Camberwell, May 3.
Messrs Baylee and Co.—Unredeemed pledges, including diamond and gold jewellery, watches, etc., at rooms, 526 Collins street, May 5, at 11 a.m.
Mr Haynes and Messrs Hill and Son—Allotments, Deepdene Tramway Estate, May 3.
Messrs Duncan and Weller—Weatherboard villa and tiled villa, Surrey Hills, May 3, at 2 p.m.

THIS MORNING

(By Our Special Representative)

LONDON, April 28.

According to the Geneva correspondent of "The Daily Express," Austrian and German aristocrats are swarming to the gambling centre at Campione, in the Como district in North Italy. The most notorious plunger at roulette is Prince Joachim, youngest son of the former Kaiser.

Owing to the nearness of Campione to the Swiss border, Swiss Deputies are urging the Federal authorities to send a protest to Rome.

paign for the sale of War Savings tificates.

Mr Barnes, Minister for Railways will leave Melbourne tomorrow morning to open the railway line Nayook to Noojee. On Friday noon Mr Clarke, Minister for Lands and Water Supply, will go to Maffra district to inquire into Boisdale irrigation project.

There arrived in Melbourne yesterday's express from Adelaide Madame Clara Serena, a well-known contralto, and her husband, Mr Mellish, who are taking a concert pany through the East and to land. Both are natives of Adelaide and were given a warm farewell many musical people. Madame Serena achieved European prominence owing to the extraordinary range power of her voice.

Dr. J. S. C. Elkington, quarantine officer, Melbourne, who has been Port Augusta quarantine camp, view to ascertaining the conditions which prevail there, returned to bourne by the Adelaide express.

Mr John Fisken, of Fisken and Company, stock and station agents, who suddenly became ill recently, is still in hospital in a critical state.

Mr D. Bruce Patterson, secretary the Associated Stock Agents, came ill on Good Friday, died last from influenza. Mr A. M'Lellan, tioneer for M'Pherson, Thom and pany, also died last evening after brief illness.

It is announced that the Right Henry W. Cleary, D.D., R Catholic Bishop of Auckland, who critically ill last week, has slightly improved.

After 44 years' service in the cation Department, Mr W. L. Richardson, head teacher of the State High street, Prahran, will retire morrow. He served in several schools throughout Victoria, including rat and Bendigo. Before taking at High street, Prahran, he was master for six years at the Violet school, Bendigo. He is in his year.

Major W. T. B. M'Cormack, who turned recently from the front, service with the Engineering will resume duty as a member Country Roads Board on Thursday has been given a cordial welcome home by Ministers, members of Parliament, and officers of the State Service.

Reuter's correspondent at Simla Admiral of the Fleet Viscount J and staff have arrived at Bombay will be entertained at a banquet United Services Club.

No action has yet been taken State Ministry to fill the vacant tions of Honorary Ministers and tary to the Cabinet (Whip). Mr Robertson, who held both position signed recently. In political circles it is thought that one member of Legislative Assembly will be appointed an Honorary Minister and a Whip. Mr Pennington may be as Whip. As none of the three vincial cities is represented in Ministry, it may be decided to an offer of the honorary portfolio Mr Duncan M'Lennan, who represent Barwon, the adjoining constituency Geelong, and is a recognised representative.

SALUTING THE FLAG IN HONOR OF AUSTRALIA'S SOLDIERS

CHILDREN OF EASTERN ROAD SCHOOL ON CEREMONIAL PARADE

Rally Behind... Which Flag?

OPPOSITE:
Children of Eastern Road School on ceremonial parade.
The Melbourne Herald, *29 April 1919.*

School children salute the Union Jack, honouring Australian dead on the first Anzac Day, 1919.

ABOVE:
Honour Roll from World War I.

This Honour Roll is displayed with pride at the Ashfield Bowling Club, New South Wales.

RIGHT:
Raising the flag at Tarakan, 1942.

An Aussie digger's hat sits above the Union Jack. The diggers at 235 Supply Depot Platoon have made their own improvized Aussie flag with a curious reversal of vexilogical protocol.

(Courtesy Australian War Memorial)

Rally Behind... Which Flag?

ABOVE:
Diggers of the 2nd A.I.F. carry the flag into battle, 1940.
(Courtesy La Trobe Library, State Library of Victoria)

OPPOSITE:
This photograph dated 23 June 1945 shows two officers of the Netherlands East Indies Army displaying a tattered Union Jack which bears the names of Australian who died on the island of Labuan, North Borneo, whilst prisoners-of-war of the Japanese.
(Courtesy Australian War Memorial)

ABOVE:
Poster from World War II.
The nations of the old empire fought together to defend King and Country—beneath the Union Jack. *Clockwise from top left:* the African colonies, India and the sub-continent, New Zealand, Britain, Australia, Canada and South Africa.
(Courtesy A. K. Macdougall)

ABOVE:
Raising the digger's hat, Tobruk, 1941.
On the morning of 22 January 1941, 1500 Italian officers and men surrendered to two Aussie brigadiers and a handful of diggers.

After hauling down the Italian flag from Admiral Massimiliano's headquarters, Corporal Eldrick Grant climbed the mast, and in the absence of any official flag hoisted his 'slouch hat' to the top. This 'flag' marked the victory as definitely, 'dinki-di Australian'.

(Courtesy Australian War Memorial)

OPPOSITE:
Bangkok, Thailand, 1945.
Australian prisoners-of-war celebrate their release with a flag made while imprisoned at No. 8 Camp, Saigon.

The flag was made from materials at hand in the camp — mosquito nets, cholera belts and loin cloths — and sewn on a machine borrowed from their Korean guards.

This photograph, taken by Lieutenant N.B. Stuckey, was taken at Bangkok airport as the ex-prisoners awaited a flight on to Singapore.

It was also an Australian ensign, made in secret by Australian prisoners-of-war, that was the first allied flag raised in Singapore after the defeat and surrender of the Japanese in 1945.

(Courtesy Australian War Memorial)

ABOVE:
For King and Country. Soldiers take a break in the officers' mess, c. 1945.
A portrait of the King is flanked by the flags of the imperial forces. There is never any doubt about who the Aussies were fighting for: King first! Country second!

(Courtesy La Trobe Library, State Library of Victoria)

ABOVE:
Manufacturing flags, Sydney, World War II.
A group of volunteers are seen making flags and adding their signatures and good wishes to flags to be sent to diggers serving overseas.

Flags were also sold by Red Cross volunteers collecting money for the Australian Comforts Fund on special 'flag days'.

(Courtesy La Trobe Library, State Library of Victoria)

'Just to add to the confusion'

In the middle of the World War II, the conservative government used the image (shown at right) of the popular, conservative British leader, Winston Churchill, to encourage voters to cast their votes for the established Australian government candidates. The Union Jack flies ahead of the Australian flag in what would seem today to be a curious reversal of symbolism.

The conservatives were returned but Menzies was replaced by Labor leader John Curtin twelve months later when Menzies was eager to go to England to work with the British War Office. Menzies often acted as a benevolent dictator; he didn't bother to discuss with cabinet several of the most important decisions which affected the Australian people.

When he took it upon himself to do his 'most melancholy duty', his declaration of war in 1939, he responded immediately to Britain's action in his broadcast to the nation ... 'Great Britain has declared war on [Germany], and as a result Australia is also at war.'

Menzies attempted to ban the Australian Communist Party but was never able to get his Bill through Parliament. His decision to change the flag from red to blue may well stem from his hatred of Communism.

An extract from his book *Afternoon Light* may shed some light on his decision: 'in the year of my birth, 1894, Queen Victoria was on the throne of the United Kingdom and Ireland and the Dominions and Colonies ... for us, the maps of the world were patterned with great areas of red, *at a time when red was a respectable colour.*'

ABOVE:

Flags of the Empire.
From *Pears Encyclopedia* 1923.

It is interesting to note how many flags featured the Union Jack in the canton, in the first half of the twentieth century before the Commonwealth started to come apart.

(Courtesy La Trobe Library, State Library of Victoria)

ABOVE LEFT:

Election campaign advertisement published in the Melbourne Herald, *10 September 1940.*

Flying the flag at R.A.F. Fighter Station in England, World War II.

A group of Australian parliamentarians pose with pilots and ground crews of an Australian squadron at the Royal Air Force fighter station in England, c. 1943.

(Courtesy La Trobe Library, State Library of Victoria)

LEFT:
Major-General 'Bloody George' Vasey raises the Australian flag over the village of Kokoda on 3 November 1943.

After six weeks of fierce battle against a battle-wearied Japanese army, the diggers finally defeated the mud and rain of the hellish Kokoda trail and walked into the village without a single shot fired at them.

The Japanese had already retreated after losing thousands of men to 'Aussie fire', disease and starvation.

(Courtesy Australian War Memorial)

OPPOSITE:
VE Day in Melbourne, 1945.
Oil painting by George Browning.

A crowd is captured gathering on the corner of Swanston and Flinders streets in Melbourne, after a thanksgiving service at St. Paul's Cathedral to celebrate the end of the war in Europe.

There are several flags of the allies on display, including the Stars and Stripes and the Union Jack. The Australian Red Ensign flies alone from a pole outside the cathedral.

(Courtesy Australian War Memorial)

The Australian Flag ~ The First 100 Years

LEFT:

Victory parade in Melbourne, 1945.

A public parade was held in the streets of Melbourne to welcome home returned A.I.F. (Australian Imperial Force) veterans.

This car was decorated with the 'official' flag of the British Empire—the Union Jack.

(Courtesy Australian War Memorial)

ABOVE:

Victory Flags for sale, c. 1940.

Two lasses in Red Cross uniforms offer Aussie victory flags for sale in aid of the Australian Comforts Fund.

(Courtesy La Trobe Library, State Library of Victoria)

Rally Behind... Which Flag?

RIGHT:
Members of the Australian battalion raise the flag, Korea, 1951.

W. J. Harrison of East Coburg in Victoria raises the flag for the first time over the snow-covered camp.

As the Australians were in Korea as part of a United Nations international force the flag was not a banner to be carried into battle. Here the flag lets the rest of the world know what sort of fighting man was to be found trying to keep warm inside these huts.

(Courtesy La Trobe Library, State Library of Victoria)

'Still confused?'

When Labor Prime Minister Paul Keating was about to launch his 1993 re-election campaign at the Balmain Sports Club he took the stage before a shimmering but plain blue curtain.

Baz Luhmann, the *énfant terrible* of the Australian movie world had been asked to prepare the stage for Keating's call to the true believers.

Keating's former speechwriter Don Watson recalled the impact of Luhmann's initial design, which also had the stars of the Southern Cross on the blue curtain:

> he showed the model . . . in a room at the Ramada. It was modest in size, simple in design, utterly arresting and breathtakingly bold. At first sight it caused the eyes to well tears and veins to bulge with national sentiment we did not know we owned. It was the most perfect and least prolix statement of a country's hope, aspiration and promise; a glimpse of what could be in a new world country not at the mercy of the past, or prey to fear, prejudice and manipulation.
>
> As soon as we saw it, we knew it was hopeless. Hogg was the first to say so. Australians would think Keating was standing in front of the flag he intended to impose on them. And if they did not think this the Opposition would certainly tell them they should think it . . .[1]

1. *Recollections of a Bleeding Heart: A Portrait of Paul Keating PM.* pages 307-8.

ABOVE:
Australian Labor Party badges from the 1985 Federal Election.

(Author's Collection)

BELOW:
The *Australian Labor Party* has used an adaption of the Australian National Flag as part of its corporate symbol, c. 2000.

BELOW:
The *Australian Liberal Party* uses a bit more of the flag as part of its corporate symbol, retaining all of that design in the top left corner.

ABOVE:
Former *One Nation Party* leader Pauline Hanson also appropriated the flag when appealing to the nation.

(Courtesy John Pasquarelli)

Rally Behind... Which Flag?

RIGHT:
Image for a dead man.
Painting by Vietnam veteran, artist Ray Beattie, acrylic on canvas and collage, 1980.

This sad, yet enigmatic image combines the well-recognized symbols of Australia's military since Gallipoli — the slouch hat, the khaki uniform and a folded Red Ensign.

(Courtesy Australian War Memorial)

ABOVE AND RIGHT:
Just a little test!

The crest above looks familiar, and the flag certainly does. However, it is not an Australian crest at all.

Take a look at the coloured crest reproduced at right and you will instantly recognize its nationality.

Yes! It is the crest of our nearest and dearest neighbour.

Still confused ... the rest of the world is too.

When then Australian Prime Minister Robert J. Hawke visited Ottawa in 1985 the Canadians raised the New Zealand flag in his honour.

The Australian Flag ~ The First 100 Years

OPPOSITE:
Greetings from Australia!
Souvenir postcard showing a flag painted onto corrugated iron, giving the illusion of a fluttering standard.
(Courtesy Portal Aird Publications, Forestville South Australia)

FAR RIGHT:
Souvenir fridge magnet, c. 2001.
This strange little koala clings to his gum-tree, wearing his little Aussie flag boxer shorts.
   He appears to be climbing out of his Aussie flag sleeping bag.
   What a concept?
   Who knows what inspires such objects, except patriotism, and an eye to making a quick dollar. The souvenir shops are filled with such nonsensical items.
(Author's collection)

JUST FOR FUN

At the dawn of the 21st century the Australian flag has discovered a new popularity, even amongst many who previously favoured its abandonment. There have been countless attempts at re-design with competitions held in national newspapers and on websites; popular personalities, country singers, sporting heroes have all had a go—but the flag remains unchanged.

In 1999 a referendum was held which gave the Australian people the opportunity to vote for constitutional change. At last! A republic—Yes or No! The Australian people overwhelmingly voted 'No!'. The 'Yes' case was supported by these same media personalities, sports stars, pop singers, eminent lawyers, academics and even politicians from the conservative side of politics, but the cause for change was lost in a climate of confusion and fear.

In a society that seemed ready to embrace its independent destiny, a community irreverent of authority, free-wheeling, fun-loving, energetic and brash, self-effacing and proud of its home-grown heroes with a good dose of the larrikin spirit thrown in, it seems astonishing the conservatives won the day.

The conservatives, the constitutional monarchists and royalists, had, as a red-herring, thrown the question of the flag into the ring in order to gain support for their cause. They suggested that the republicans also wanted to change the flag. While it may be true—many who favoured constitutional change may also have favoured a change to the flag—this issue was not relevant to the terms of the referendum.

It was apparent at the Sydney Olympics held the following year that the Aussie flag had at last come into its own. Aussies couldn't get enough of it. The Australian people had at last taken the old Blue Ensign to heart, as well as to its head, its chest, its bulging biceps, its bottoms, bellies and bras. The Aussies proudly flew the striking colours to show off to the world, again and again and again—and it was all great fun!

Can't get enough of that empire!

ABOVE:
Souvenir fan, c. 1953.
Issued by a Sydney department store in celebration of the visit of Queen Elizabeth II to Australia in 1953, the first visit to Australia's shores by a ruling monarch.

(Author's collection)

BELOW:
Lucky Hit tobacco tin.
The ubiquitous tobacco tin could be found filled with nails, screws or rivets in almost every Australian shed and garage. No patriotic Aussie grandad ever discarded this useful symbol of British empire.

ABOVE:
'Oxo Beef Cube' commemorative tin, c. 1951.
The coronation of Queen Elizabeth II did not escape even the beef cube manufacturers.
It seems that the empire couldn't get enough of the royals, even though there is no sense whatsoever of any colonial connection in this design.

BELOW:
'I wonder how they would like it …'
Cartoon by John Allison.

OPPOSITE:
Souvenir tea caddies, c 1927.
The Duke and Duchess of York are honoured on these tins issued in commemoration of the opening of first federal parliament in Canberra on 9 May 1927.
The Australian flag is shown here as blue. This colour was reserved for government (administrative) use at this time.

(Author's collection)

The greatest sporting nation in the world!

The boxing kangaroo flag.

This origin of the design of this flag is uncertain. While some believe that it was the work of a student at West Australian Institute of Technology, others believe it to be the work of professional graphic designers from the west.

Whatever its origin it flew into international prominence when Perth businessman and entrepreneur Alan Bond took on the Yanks and won the America's Cup from them in 1983.

The boxing kangaroo soon became the unofficial sporting emblem of the Australian nation.

ABOVE:

Symbol of the Champion brand of clothing, Melbourne, 1941.

The boxing kangaroo flag is now an official Australian Olympic Committee flag and is protected against misuse and plagiarism by the committee.

It was purchased by the AOC from the receiver of Bond Corporation, after its collapse in the 1980s.

A similar design was painted on the fusilage of at least one RAAF fighter plane during World War II.

It appears that sometimes the old ideas are often still the best.

(Author's photograph)

Just for Fun

ABOVE:
Advertising poster, 1932.

Poster for a boxing match between Australian Ambrose Palmer and American Young Stribling at The Stadium, Rushcutters Bay, 4 July 1932.
 The Australian flag shown here is clearly the Red Ensign; the blue flag was not adopted for civil use until some twenty years after this event.

ABOVE:
Christmas greeting card, c. 1930.

Again the Australian flag is shown as the Red Ensign.
 It cannot be simply economy of print production that dictates the colour of these flags: red, black and blue are all available to the printer.
 The choice has been made to print the flag red as this was the accepted colour of the national (civil) flag in common use.

(Courtesy La Trobe Library, State Library of Victoria)

The Australian Flag ~ The First 100 Years

BELOW:

Parachutist Russell Lee brings a big flag to ground on Queen Elizabeth Oval in the Victorian City of Bendigo, Australia Day, 26 January 2002.

OPPOSITE, LEFT:

Media personality, broadcaster and gourmet chef, Frenchman Gabriel Gaté waves the flag as part of his role as Australia Day Ambassador to Bendigo on 26 January 2002.

(Courtesy the Bendigo Advertiser*)*

ABOVE AND RIGHT:

Bathing boxes on the foreshore at Brighton, Victoria.

All sorts of designs adorn the humble, yet highly prized, pieces of beach-front real estate on Port Phillip Bay, Victoria. From fantastic whales to Hokasai waves, and from mermaids to the Aussie flag, a wide range of Australian interests and tastes are reflected here. Yet once again the Union Jack tends to dominate with this striking design (right).

(Photographs by the Author)

RIGHT:

It has taken no small degree of concerted effort by politicians, local government and community activists to get Australians to celebrate 26 January as eagerly as the Americans do Independence Day and the French do Bastille Day.

But a century or so since federation, Aussies have finally found something worth celebrating in their usual fashion, with hundreds of breakfast barbies, beer barrels, beach cricket and bums in boxers.

It is a pity that with the cut of these undershorts these young Aussies seem to be partying in honour of the 'mother country' (England)—just as well for 'the green and gold'.

The Australian Flag ~ The First 100 Years

Cartoon by Michael Leunig.

(Courtesy, Michael Leunig and the Age newspaper)

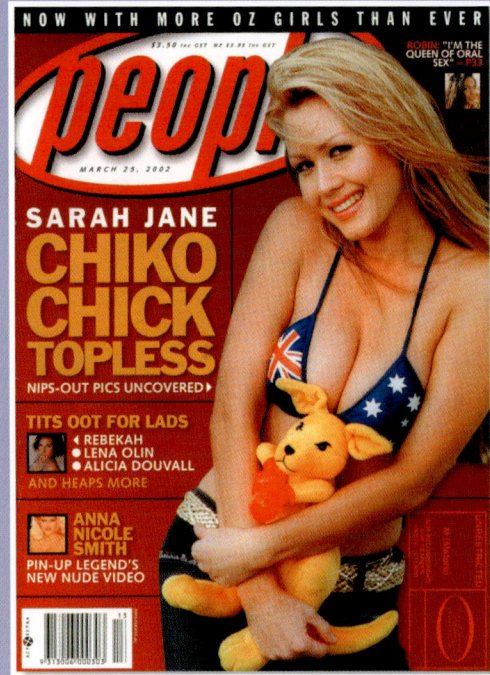

ABOVE:

Model Sarah Jane King proudly displays both the flag and the boxing Kangaroo in this cover shot for *People* magazine, 25 March 2002.

(Courtesy People *nagazine, ACP Publishing)*

Just for Fun

RIGHT:
Anzac biscuit pack, c. 2001.

Made from 'Australia's authentic recipe', these biscuits are actually approved by the Returned Services League (RSL). Nobody seems to have noticed that the Union Jack is missing from this representation of the flag.

ABOVE:
Aussie utes line up outside a country pub.

These utes display the symbols of country Australia — the Aussie flag and the yellow banner of Bundaberg Rum.

The Rebel Flag of the defeated southern army from the American Civil War (1861–65) is another of those flags of protest and independence loved by country folk, just like the Eureka flag.

(Photographs courtesy the Author)

The Australian Flag ~ The First 100 Years

Cartoon by Ron Tanberg
Published in the *Sydney Morning Herald, 19 August 1996.*

ABOVE AND LEFT:
Die-cut souvenir postcards.

(Courtesy Portal Aird Publications, Forestville South Australia)

LEFT, BELOW:
Menu from the Arab Coffee Lounge, Lorne, Victoria, c. 1969

Designer Graham Smith has altered the symbolic relationship of young Australia to Britain in this design from the swinging sixties.

The *Arab* also ran a disco called 'The Wild Colonial Boy' — another tentative step towards a republic taken by the baby boomers.

(Author's collection)

Just for Fun

RIGHT:
Souvenir gear, c. 2000.

From the incredible opening ceremony of the Sydney Olympics to the flutter of the last flag, the eyes of the world were on Australia, and the Aussies put on the 'greatest show on earth'.

It almost seems that for the first time the designs of the Aussie flag truly expressed the spirit of the nation. The deep blue of the sea and sky, the blood red of the landscape and the brilliance of the Southern Cross were all reflected here.

It seemed that we knew, for the first time that we were truly one people, with one destiny and with OUR flag!

Go Aussies.

Aussie, Aussie, Aussie, Oi! Oi! Oi!

BELOW:
'G'Day the Aussie Bear'.
A 'Beanie Kid' stuffed toy.

(Courtesy Skansen Giftware, New South Wales)

(Photograph by Colin Barr, Boxer shorts by Mitch Dowd)

Aussie! Aussie! Aussie!

The flag debate continued to rage during the Sydney Olympics. Most detractors of the Australian blue flag complained it was simply not distinctive enough when surrounded by its neighbours, or in close proximity to the flags of New Zealand or any of the scores of other 'colonial' and state flags which still bear the Union Jack in their upper left corners.

The flags of Anguilla; Bermuda; the British Virgin Islands; the Caymans, Cook, Falkland, Pitcairn, Turks and Caicos Islands; Gibraltar; Hawaii; Hong Kong; Manitoba; St. Helena; and Tuvalu could all be confused with the Australian flag when viewed from a distance.

Harold Scruby, one of the directors of *Ausflag*, wrote the following in a piece titled 'It's due time to scrap the Jack', published in the *Australian* newspaper on Australia Day 2001:

Dressing Up Mutton as Lamb: and in spite of the best publicity which can be given to any flag—the Olympic Games—our flag remains the unambiguous symbol of some unrecognisable, British branch office. A nation's flag is its supreme marketing symbol. However recent events have emerged which prove conclusively that the Australian flag is a commercial disaster.

On 24 May 2000 the Sydney *Daily Telegraph*, contributed the following to this debate:

Australian Flag a Dud: The current Australian flag is such an ambiguous symbol of our nationhood, is so uninspiring, and is so divisive, that the Australian Olympic Committee doesn't want it to be used by fans at the upcoming Sydney Olympic Games.

Olympic sports fans have been urged to use the boxing kangaroo as the team symbol of the Sydney games instead of the Australian flag. The icon is set for a resurgence this month when the Australian Olympic Committee launches nationwide sales of the battle flag.

Australian Prime Minister John Howard, flushed with the great outpouring of goodwill that followed the Olympics, suggested the games had 'put back the cause of those who want to change the flag by a generation.'

But dissenting opinions flooded in to newspapers all around the country. Just because Aussies put politics, and a century of longing, on hold for a couple of weeks in the spring of 2000 doesn't mean that the desire for change

ABOVE:

Cattlemen of the High Country parade the flag at the opening ceremony of the Sydney Olympic Games, 2000.

(Photographs courtesy Australian Associated Press)

Aussie! Aussie! Aussie!

RIGHT:

Russian-born Australian Olympian, Tatiana Grigorieva pole-vaulted her way into the hearts of all Australians when she won silver in the inaugural women's event.

This energetic and spirited young woman and her Russian-born husband, who was also on the Australian team, are typical of the new face of the Australian nation.

It may be that in the arguments for a change to the flag there lies some truth.

The Union Jack seen here, as Tatiana drapes the Australian flag around her shoulders, does little to reflect the multi-culturalism that is the contemporary Australian nation.

Maybe in the new millennium we are seeing the 150-year-old Eureka dream realized.

All peoples standing together, people of all nations, standing as one — beneath the Southern Cross.

(Photograph by Dallas Kilponen, courtesy of the Melbourne Age newspaper)

The Australian Flag ~ The First 100 Years

LEFT:

Go Aussie Go!
Spectators at the beach volleyball event, Bondi, Sydney Olympics 2000.

It is no wonder the flag debate persists without resolution. In this newspaper photograph several different flag designs are being waved, and worn, in patriotic support of the Australian team — and by the one supporter.

One correspondent to the *Sydney Morning Herald* wrote on 3 November:

> Many symbols for Australia were evident. They included our Australian flag, the boxing kangaroo, the Aboriginal flag, and faces painted in green and gold as well as red, white and blue.
>
> Certainly our present flag has served us well. Nevertheless, it is painfully obvious that it is no longer fulfilling its role, and a new design must be found to unify all Australians.

Opposite:

Spectators Trevor and Pam Cole protect themselves against the vagaries of Sydney weather with their patriotic headgear. Stadium Australia, Sydney, 15 September 2000.

(Photographs courtesy Australian Associated Press and the Melbourne Age *newspaper)*

OPPOSITE PAGE:
Fifth Place Victory!
In 2002, the Australian Grand Prix fifth-placegetters, Minardi owner Paul Stoddart and driver Mark Webber, celebrate their success with two Aussie classics, the flag and Fosters.

Even if Aussies come in the back of the pack, as long as they feature in the placings they are still our heroes.

Just as Steven Bradbury won Gold at the Salt Lake City Winter Olympics in 2002, simply by being the last man standing, the Minardi team raced to fifth place after half the pack had destroyed themselves on the first corner in the race around Albert Park.

As cars flew into the air and tore themselves apart, it was true Aussie grit and staying power that took the Minardi team over the line.

When radio commentator Phillip Adams told a group of university students in the 1970s that they should always remember 'Australia rhymes with failure', he wasn't to know that other people's failures also facilitate our successes.

Anyway, Aussies have always liked those who come second the best — or fifth!

Remember Gallipoli; our greatest defeat has become our historically defining moment.

Our failure often begets our success.

(Photograph courtesy of Australian Associated Press)

Victory Lap!
The flag is taken for a victory lap at the Australian Motorcycle Grand Prix 1996.

(Photograph courtesy Australian Associated Press)

has gone away. The evidence is expressed in this letter by Andrew Parker of the Australian Capital Territory to the *Sydney Morning Herald*, 29 September 2000:

> The Sydney Olympics have been a success because they have showcased contemporary Australia, our culture and its uniqueness. A unique people, a unique city; a unique nation! The exception is our flag. It is a cheap relic of the past that sends all the wrong signals to our people and our overseas visitors. Like our head of state, our flag should be unambiguously Australian.
>
> The Union Jack, with Southern Cross attached, has had more PR and prime time than anything else in these Games; a billion dollar sponsorship package for free; but you can't sell a lemon . . .

The search for one symbol that will truly unite 'one people, one destiny' remains an undercurrent of Australian life. Maybe the Australians are happy with a whole range of symbols that neither truly define them nor excludes them.

The contemporary society that is Australia in the 21st century may not need one fluttering symbol to rally behind, because it almost seems to adopt anything going and waves that as well. Is this true democracy at work? Or are Aussies just scared of having to make a big decision all by themselves?

Maybe it is better just to let things be and somewhere along the line it will just evolve anyway, or someone who knows what they are doing will sort it all out for them.

For Australians in the 21st century it seems that slow evolution beats revolution any day. Just look at how long it took them to get the first flag organized—Ah well! What's the big hurry anyway?

Left:

Gold in 'them thar hills!'

Golden girl Alisa Camplin celebrates her win in the aerial freestyle event at Salt Lake City, Winter Olympics 2002.

Once again the Union Jack dominates Australia's victory.

(Photograph courtesy of the Age newspaper)

Opposite:

Stamping his name across the world!

On centre court at Wimbledon in June 2002, Lleyton Hewitt, the 'bad-boy' of Australian tennis smashed his way into the finals and ultimately finished to be the world's number one.

Once again the stalls were filled with fluttering flags, but with the Union Jack in the corner of the Aussie flag it was at times difficult to tell who was supporting who.

Australia Post released this special collectors' edition of postage stamps featuring a portrait of Australia's latest number one hero alongside the flag and a very robust looking 'big red' kangaroo.

It is interesting to note that the flag on the stamps is cropped cleverly, to show the Southern Cross dominating the Union Jack — after all this Aussie certainly dominated the Poms, and everybody else, in the English summer of 2002.

Aussie! Aussie! Aussie!
Yeah! Yeah! Yeah!

(National Philatelic Collection, Australia Post)

Aussie! Aussie! Aussie!

FLAGS OF THE NATION

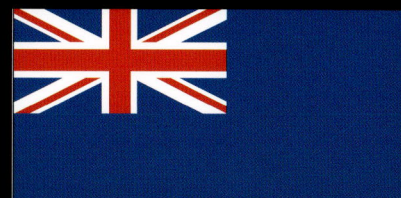

The British Blue Ensign.

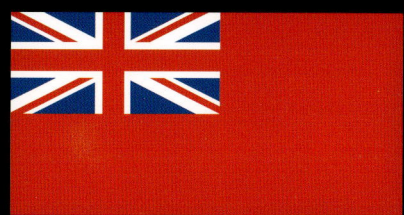

The British Red Ensign.

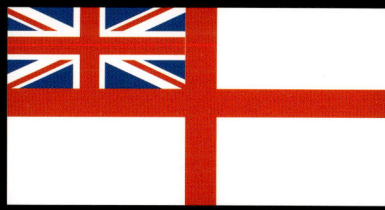

The British White Ensign.

OPPOSITE:

Empire Day. Newstead, Victoria, 1915.
Patriotic citizens of the small Victorian rural community of Newstead gather to salute the flags of empire.
There is no doubt about which flag is the more prominent on this proud day.

(Courtesy Newstead Historical Society)

The flag we so proudly hold as our own is not at all remarkable in its design. With due respect to the wishes of the judging panel of the Federation Flag Competition, the flag has simply added the stars of the constellation to the established colours of the British red and blue ensigns. Even the earlier Federation Flag adapted the existing design of the British White Ensign, by changing the colour of the saltire of St. George and adding the Southern Cross.

Was there ever any other possibility of any other solution at all?

The *Herald* Newspaper certainly thought so at the time. They expressed their dislike for a flag that showed so little originality and creativity in its design, and offered their own design in its place. It appears that they were keen to distance Australia from its British colonial past and embrace the attitudes of the 'new world' by proposing a design that looked curiously American.

The Australian Blue Ensign, 1901.

The Australian Red Ensign, 1901.

The Herald *Design, 1901.*

The Union Flag and the Union Jack

It was the Union Flag of Queen Anne that was first flown on Australian soil, when Captain James Cook raised the flag at Botany Bay on 29 April 1770.

The design of the Union Jack flag represents the union of nations within the British Isles: the St. George Cross of England, the Saltire of St. Andrew representing Scotland and the Saltire of St. Patrick representing Ireland (which was added to the Union Flag in January 1801).

After this addition in 1801, the flag was known as the Union Jack, taking this name from a 'jack' which is the common name for a flag flown from the jackstaff (a short flagpole at the stern of a ship) when a ship is in port.

The placement of the saltires within the Union Jack design are a constant reminder to the nations represented here — England dominates Scotland and Ireland is the inferior. When placed on the Australian flag the symbolism of the Union Jack becomes even more striking.

Queen Anne Union Flag.
This flag was first adopted on 12 April 1606 in the United Kingdom. It was first flown in Australia by Captain James Cook on 29 April 1770, and later by Captain Arthur Phillip (the colony's first governor) on 26 January 1788.

St. George Cross.
This component of the Union Flag and later the Union Jack represents England.

Saltire of St. Andrew.
This component of the Union Flag and later the Union Jack represents Scotland.

Saltire of St. Patrick.
This banner representing Ireland was added to the Union Flag in 1801, after which the flag became known as the Union Jack.

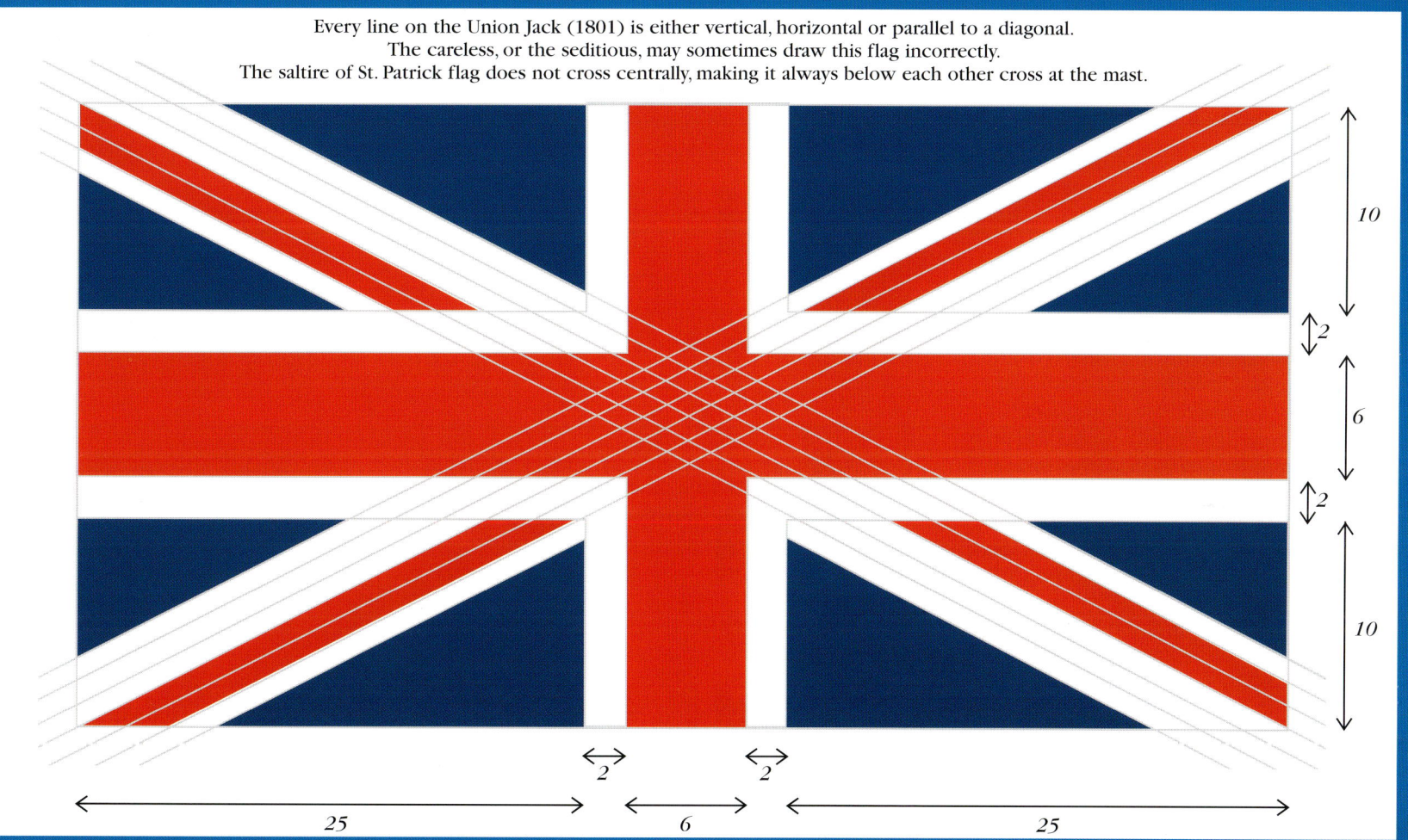

How to draw the Union Jack — just in case!

The Australian National Flags

After Australia's federation in 1901 the Australian government commissioned the designs shown at right.

The Red Ensign was intended as a merchant flag, to be flown on merchants ships registered in Australia, and the flag of Australian citizens at sea. Citizens on land were expected to continue to fly the Union Jack.

The red flag soon became the *unofficial* civil ensign and the *unofficial* national flag on land. The Union Jack remained the official Australian civil flag.

The blue flag was reserved solely for government use; it was rarely flown as the Union Jack took precedence at almost all official occasions.

It is described as a *defaced* British Blue Ensign, just as the red flag is similarly described as a *defaced* British Red Ensign.

The British ensigns were still seen as dominant over these colonial flags. By adapting their designs Australia had *defaced* them, not added to them or made them better, but rather diminished them.

Flags of the Nation

Red Ensign (Civil and Merchant).
Adopted in Australia on 3 September 1901 this design was based on the British Red Ensign defaced with a design of the Southern Cross in the fly.
The six-starred Federation Star points directly to the Union Jack.
The other stars are irregular in design, having from five to nine points, in an attempt to represent the apparent brightness of each in the night sky.

Blue Ensign (Government).
Adopted in Australia on 3 September 1901 for government use.

1901

Red Ensign (Civil and Merchant).
To aid ease of manufacture the larger stars of the Southern Cross were modified to all be the same size and design.
The smaller star retained only five points.
This revised design was adopted by Australia on 20 February 1903.

Blue Ensign (Government).
This revised design of the Blue Ensign (showing modified stars) was adopted on 20 February 1903.

1903

Red Ensign (Civil and Merchant).
The flag was altered again and adopted on 22 May 1909 after Australia had gained the Territory of Papua in 1906.
Although the Northern Territory and Australian Capital Territory were also added to the territories of Australia in 1911, it was decided not to change the flag again and to acknowledge all territories added after 1911 through the seventh point of the Federation Star.
The Red Ensign became the unofficial National Flag until it was replaced by the official Blue Ensign in 1954.

22 May 1909-1941: Government use only.
1954: Australian National Flag.
This Blue Ensign became the official Australian National Flag in 1954. Prime Minister Robert G. Menzies simply changed the civil for the administrative.

1909/1954

Flags of the States

Up until federation each separate colony had its own laws, customs and economy. Even the gauge of railway lines were different, making interstate travel and commerce a less than efficient system.

The postcard shown at right illustrates a contemporary view of the prosperity ahead for Australia after the artificiality of colonial borders were torn down—all Australians together benefitting from one common wealth.

Each new state, however, retained its individual identity through its own ceremonial designs as indicated in the page opposite.

Each of the flags is described as *defaced* British blue ensigns upon which Victoria carries the stars of the Southern Cross beneath an Imperial Crown, New South Wales carries the Cross of St. George and the Imperial Lion, and Tasmania carries its Lion.

South Australia has one of the few emblems that reflect Australian fauna with its magpie. For no apparent reason Queensland has a Cross of the Knights of Malta and Crown, while Western Australia carries the black swan, as it has since 1870 when the colony was known as the Swan River Settlement.

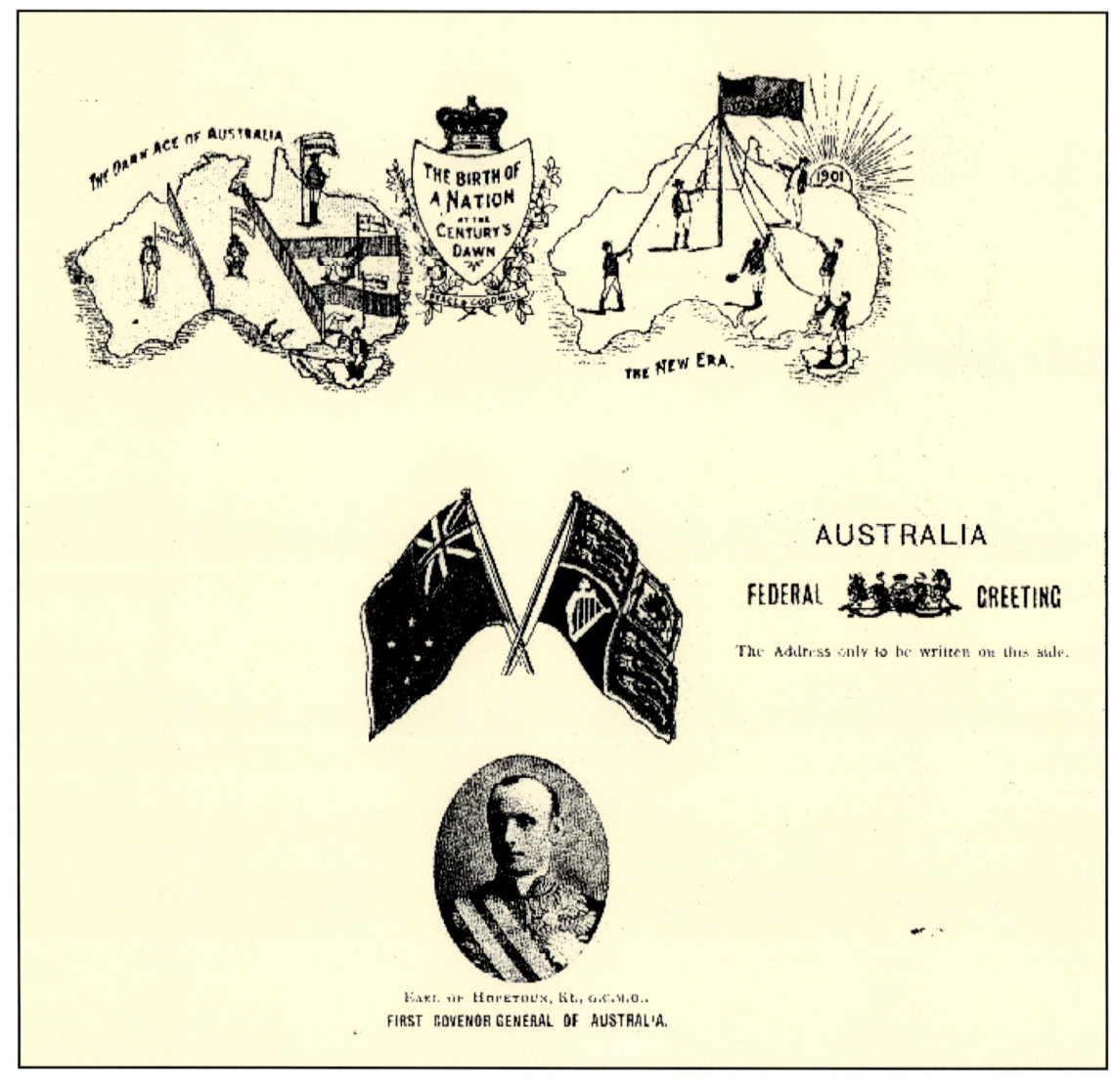

Flags of the Nation

Victorian Flag.
Adopted 21 March 1877.

The State badge of Victoria depicts the Southern Cross surmounted by the St. Edwards Crown. The stars in the Southern Cross range from five to eight points.

The design of the crown can change with a change of monarch; the last was in 1953 after Queen Elizabeth II adopted the St. Edwards Crown following her Coronation in 1953.

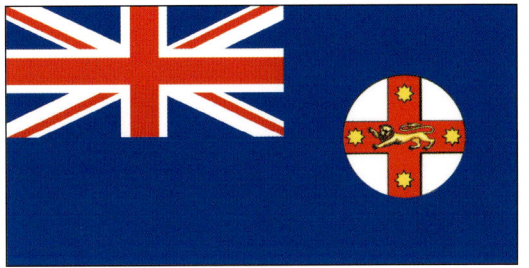

Tasmanian Flag.
Adopted 29 November 1875.

The flag of Tasmania depicts a red lion passant on a white disc.

The exact symbolism of the badge is unknown, other than to indicate historical ties with England.

The badge was approved by the British Colonial Office in 1875 and the design of the Tasmanian flag has remained unchanged since then, other than a slight alteration made to the lion in 1975.

Queensland Flag.
Adopted 23 March 1876.

When Queensland Colonial Secretary and Treasurer William Hemmant designed the original state badge, no reason was offered for his decision to use the Maltese Cross as the emblem. It is often suggested that the concept was inspired by the Victoria Cross, Britain's highest award for bravery.

The cross has a St. Edwards Crown at its centre. As in Victoria, this flag can change with a change of monarch. The current version was introduced in 1953.

New South Wales Flag.
Adopted 18 February 1876.

This flag bears the cross of St. George in red on a white disc. An eight-pointed star sits on each arm of the cross at whose centre is a lion passant.

This flag was designed by colonial architect James Barnet and retired Royal Navy Captain Francis Hixson.

There is a move afoot to replace this design with a flag that better reflects contemporary New South Wales.

South Australian Flag.
Adopted 13 January 1904.

A white-backed piping shrike (magpie), wings outstretched, against a yellow disc makes the flag of South Australia one of the few state flags that actually reflects Australian fauna.

This flag designed by Robert Craig of the Adelaide School of Arts replaced the earlier complicated design of the state badge, which showed Brittania in conversation within an indigenous Australian. The old design was considered to difficult to reproduce.

Western Australian Flag.
Adopted c.1953.

The decision to take the black swan as the emblem for Western Australia stems from 1870 when the western state was known as the Swan River Settlement.

Governor Weld suggested then that the black swan was the obvious choice for the badge of the colony.

Like South Australia, the west is represented by a truly Australian icon, not an imperial one.

The Aboriginal flag

This distinctive flag, designed by Arrente (Central Australia) artist Harold Thomas, was first flown on 12 July 1971 on National Aboriginal and Islander Day in Adelaide.

Thomas felt that the Aboriginal people needed a unifying symbol they could claim as their own. He remarked upon the plethora of symbols carried at protests and marches that all represented a European identity. He felt: 'We needed a common symbol to march with, as blacks together in unity, and something we could be proud of.' Today, this flag is often carried by Europeans who also see the design as representative of a truly Australian national identity, irrespective of skin colour.

Harold's design is expressed this way: 'the red panel represents the land; the black represents the people; the gold represents the sun, the giver of life.'

On 14 July 1995, the Aboriginal flag was proclaimed as an official Australian flag for the nation's indigenous people.

Flags of the Territories

Australia has responsibility for a number of territories from small island groups, the seat of national government (Australian Capital Territory, ACT), the Antarctic and the large state-sized chunk of land known as the Northern Territory.

The Prime Minister of Australia John Howard, attempted to make the issue of statehood for the Northern Territory an electoral bargaining chip in the 1996 Federal election, but the people of the territory voted a resounding — *NO!*

Northern Territory Flag. Adopted 1 July 1978.
The Northern Territory was founded as a Federal Territory at the same time as the ACT; however, this flag was not hoisted until self-government was granted on 1 January 1978.

The flag was designed by Victorian artist Robert Ingpen and features both terittorian colours and a symbolic form of Sturt's desert rose.

The Southern Cross is the Victorian version with the number of points on the stars varying from five to eight.

Flags of the Nation

The territorians, ever distrustful of the carpet-baggers from the south, just thought there were too many strings attached. They were happy enough with things the way they were.

However, all of the territories do have a strong sense of pride in their very special place and the design of their flag certainly indicates their sense of individuality.

The flags of most of the territories reflect a contemporary view, informed by geography and habitat, not by ideas of political prowess, status or imperial traditions.

Norfolk Island Flag.
Adopted 17 January 1980.

Norfolk Island has been an Australian external territory since 1905.

It has had its own legislative assembly since 1979, and since then has flown its own distinctive flag.

The green stripes represent the abundant vegetation on the island with the silhouette of the well-recognized Norfolk Island pine tree set against the centre white panel.

Australian Capital Territory Flag.
Adopted 25 March 1993.

The Australian Capital Territory (ACT) was founded as a federal territory on 1 January 1911, and attained self-government on 4 March 1989; however it took until 25 March 1993 for the territory to finally have its own flag.

This design, by Ivo Ostyn, replaces a similar design which had an ochre-red background, used by the city of Canberra.

The crest in the centre is a modified form of the arms of the City of Canberra.

Christmas and Cocos Islands Flag.

This flag was designed by mining supervisor Tony Couch of Sydney, and was unofficially adopted on 14 April 1986. Tony received a $100 prize for his design.

The blue triangle represents the sea, the green and the vegetation covering the island. In the green triangle is a symbol of the golden bosun bird which is unique to the islands.

The golden circle with the map represents Christmas Island's phosphate mining history.

Torres Strait Islands Flag.

The Torres Strait Islander flag was designed by Bernard Namok and adopted in 1992.

Green represents the islands, blue the sea, and black the local Melanesian people. A stylized dancer's headdress (dari), and a five-pointed star appear on the flag.

The star represents the five main island zones and is sometimes interpreted as a symbol of the 'coming of the light' to the islanders—the coming of Christianity.

On 14 July 1995, this flag was proclaimed the official flag for the indigenous Torres Strait Islanders.

Flags of the Services

Diggers on leave in London show the flag, c. 1917.

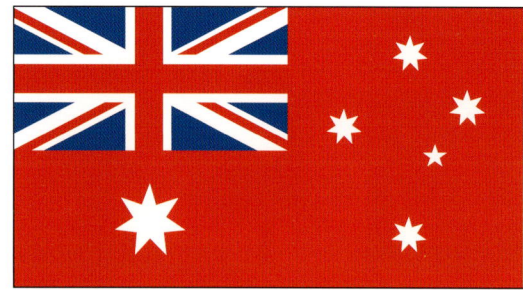

Australian Red Ensign.

The Australian Army, unlike the other armed forces, does not have its own ensign; however it is charged with the defence of the Australian National Flag (Blue Ensign), and therefore flies the national flag as its own.

The Red Ensign has been the flag of Australian registered ships since 1981.

Ensign of the Royal Australian Air Force.

The RAAF ensign was gained the imperial approval of King George VI in 1948 and was first used in Australia in 1949.

The red kangaroo was added to the roundel in 1982.

Murray Rivers Flag.

The Murray Rivers flag was flown on paddlesteamers that plied the river trade in the 1850s. It is still flown today on craft that use the mighty Murray.

Curiously enough, the blue stripes are meant to represent the flowing waters of that mighty watercourse; what a pity that the river is almost a permanent shade of muddy brown.

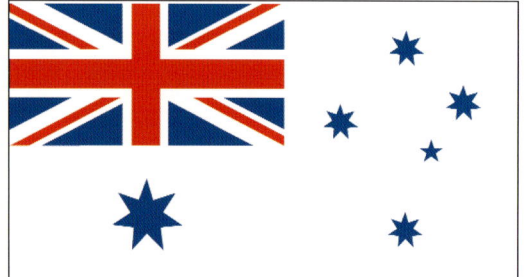

Australian White Ensign.

The naval ensign was changed to this design during the Vietnam War in 1967.

This flag was previously the same design as the British White Ensign.

The British complained that their ships were being mistaken for Australian vessels and were being attacked in the South China seas.

The confusion over symbols can sometimes be a matter of life or death.

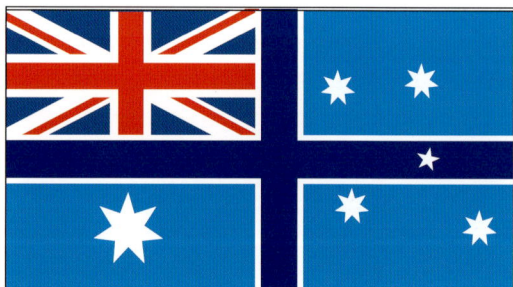

The Civil Aviation Ensign of Australia.

The Civil Air ensign was first adopted in 1935. This flag represents the Commonwealth organization responsible for civil aviation, and is flown at airports, boats, on government buildings and aircraft.

The flag initially had yellow stars but these were changed to white in 1947 to make them easier to read from long distance.

New Ideas!

Australian artist and designer Ken Done was asked in 1995 by then Prime Minister Paul Keating to develop some designs for a new flag.

The Lord Mayor of Sydney endorsed the idea of making-up and flying some of these designs around Sydney. Ken Done donated some funds to Ausflag for this display.

Three of the designs were produced and were officially raised on 28 January 1996, with 150 flags flying over Sydney. Radio station 2-Day-FM conducted a phone-in survey to gauge the public reaction.

There have been many others as well as Done who continue to stretch their imaginations in the search for the ultimate new Australian Flag.

Shown at right are just some of the hundreds of designs, from literally hundreds of both professional and amateur designers, that continue to flourish right across the 'wide brown land.'

The design at bottom right is certainly suggestive of that ancient concept, although it does look a bit like the stars are swimming in mud!

LEFT COLUMN:
Three designs by Ken Done based on the Southern Cross.

(Reproduced courtesy of Harold Scruby, Ausflag)

TOP CENTRE:
Design by Ken Done based on the Federation Star.

SECOND ROW, CENTRE:
Design by Ken Done based on the Anzac badge, the 'Rising Sun'.

THIRD ROW, CENTRE
Fauna design by Ken Done.

TOP RIGHT:
Design by Mark Tucker.

SECOND ROW, RIGHT:
Adaptation by Ausflag's Harold Scruby.

THIRD ROW, RIGHT
The Wide Brown Land flag.

Flag Protocol

While any person may fly a flag there are rules (protocol) which ensure that the national symbol is treated with respect at all times.

The blue Australian flag is the correct flag to fly on land, and although the Red Ensign is the correct flag that should be flown by Australian registered ships, the Blue Ensign may also be flown, but the two are never to be flown at the same time or on the same vessel.

Government policy stresses that the flag should not be defaced in any way and that it is improper to use it in certain ways, such as a table or seat cover; a covering for a statue, monument or plaque at an unveiling ceremony; a mask for boxes, barriers or draped below a table on a dias or platform. The flag should not be allowed to fall or lie on the ground.

The flag should only be used for advertising purposes in a dignified manner, and should be depicted 'aloft and free'.

It seems that Australians regard their national banner in the same way they treat almost everything else, with scant regard for protocol and government decree but strongy felt patriotism, deep affection and larrikin amusement.

Just look at how the Aussies have treated their flag: they have turned it into bras and panties, boxers shorts, doona covers, toilet seats and t-shirts, tea towels and table cloths, car seat covers and ankle sox — the Australian ingenuity will leave no stone unturned, no marketing opportunity denied.

Dick Smith flies the flag on all his 'Aussie' products, Big Kev does the same; the flag of the Southern Cross flies on almost every aspect of Australian enterprise, as does the boxing kangaroo, the battle flag of Eureka and the Aboriginal red, yellow and black. They are all symbols that Australians will put their hand over their hearts and salute — at the appropriate time regardless of the protocol.

However, there are some occasions when even the most irreverent of Australians never fail to do the right thing.

Flying the flag at other times.

The Australian National Flag should be flown on all government buildings during normal working hours.

The flag should also be displayed at polling Places on the occasion of a national election or referendum.

Flags should not be flown upside down except as a genuine signal of distress. Two flags should never be flown on the one flag-pole.

Flying the flag at half-mast.

The flag should only be flown at half-mast as a sign of mourning. The flag should first be raised to the top of the mast then lowered slowly to the half-mast position; at the end of the day the flag should be raised to the top again before being lowered for removal.

The flag should be flow at half-mast on the following occasions:
  on the death of the *sovereign*
  on the death of a *member of the royal family*
  on the death of the *governor-general* or *past governor-general*
  on the death of a *distinguished Australian citizen*
  on the death of a *foreign sovereign or head of state.*

The flag may also be flown at half-mast on the death of a local citizen in accordance with the wishes of the local community; however the flag should only be at half-mast at the place where the citizen is laying in state, all other flags in that community should be at full-mast.

A flag may be used to cover the coffin of a distinguished person. The upper left quarter of the flag should be placed above the head of the coffin, over the heart.

Commemoration Days

Flags are always flown on the following days:

1 January - Anniversary of the establishment of the *Commonwealth of Australia.*

26 January - *Australia Day.*
The flag should also be flown on the Monday holiday associated with Australia Day.

Second Monday in March - *Commonwealth Day.*

25 April - *Anzac Day.*
Flags are to be flown at half-mast until noon.

9 May - Anniversary of the *inauguration of Canberra* (Canberra only).

June - The official *birthday of the Sovereign.* The date is announced annually with the second Monday given as the Queen's Birthday public holiday. This holiday is celebrated in October in Western Australia.

July - *NAIDOC (National Aboriginal and Islander's Day Observation Committee) week.* The Aboriginal flag and the Torres Strait Islander flag should be flown during this week but should not replace the Australian flag. They should only be flown on additional flagpoles on public buildings.

3 September - *Australian National Flag Day.*

11 November - *Remembrance Day.*
Flags should be flown at half-mast between 10.30 am and 11.03 am.

Flag Terminology

Canton: The place of honour is the upper half of a flag nearest the hoist, or first quarter.
Fly: The half of a flag farthest from the halyard.
Halyard: Side of a flag nearest the rope.
Hoist: Half of a flag closest to the halyard.
Second Quarter: Upper half of the fly.
Third Quarter: Lower half of the hoist.
Fourth Quarter: Lower half of the fly.

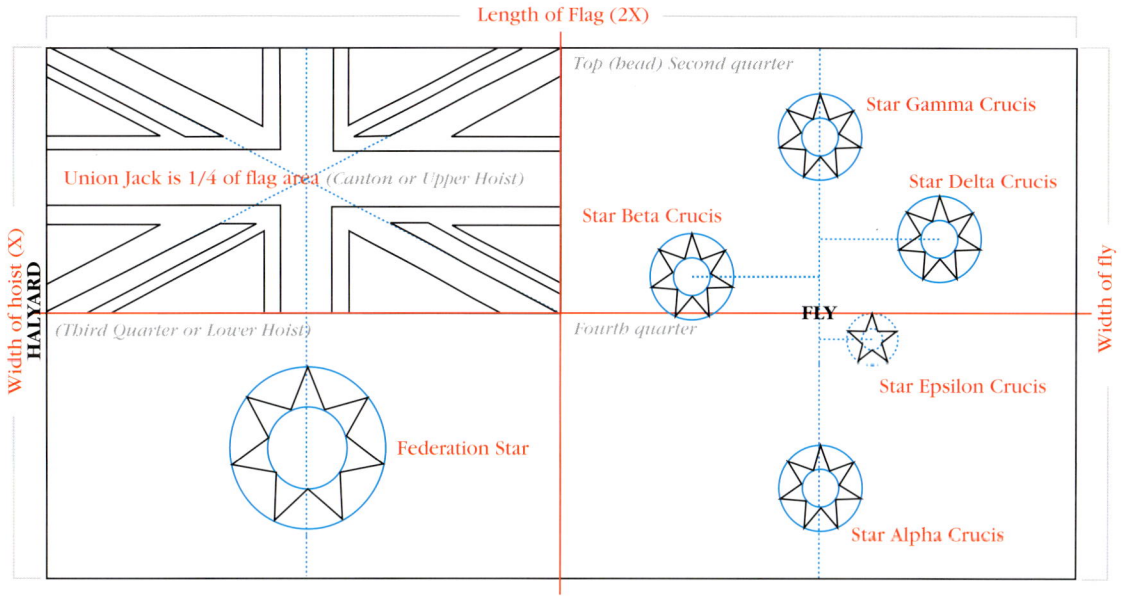

Index

Advance Australia
    Coat of arms 4, 8,
Age, The, competition 6, 54
Anti-Transportation League flag 6, 23
ANZAC 58
    biscuits 87
    cove 2
Ashfield Bowling Club 65
ATSIC 53
Australia For Ever – song sheet 38
Ausflag 51, 90
    Ausflag competition 54
    Frank Gentil 54
    Peter Lambert 54
    George Margaritis 54
    Harold Scruby 90, 109
Australia Day Poster 85
Australia House London 39
Australia Today 56
Awake! Awake! Australia –
    song sheet 38

Ballarat 6
    Fine Art Gallery 48
    mining exchange 46
    Sturt Street 51
    Subscription Ball, 9
    Reform League 51
Bangkok 66
Barton, Edmund 32
Bathing boxes, Brighton, Vic. 84
Bendigo, Victoria 6, 83
Boer War 59
Borneo 63, 64
Botany Bay 6, 19
Boxing Kangaroo flag 6, 82, 90
Bowman Flag 6
Bradbury, Steven 95
British Union Flag 6, 20, 100
Burke and Wills Burial, 11
Bulletin, The 53

Camplin, Alisa 96
Champion Brand Clothing 82
Churchill, Winston 70
Communist Party 70
competition, flag design
    Review of Reviews 28
    winners 34
Cook, Captain James 6, 20
    statue Hyde Park, Sydney 24

Digger's flag 6, 45
Done, Ken 109

Donoghue, Lois 53
Dorrington, Annie 34
Dowd, Mitch 89
Duke and Duchess of York, tea tins 81

Elizabeth II 38
    Beef cube tin 80
    sporting oval, Bendigo 85
Evans, Ivor 34
Eureka 43
    flag 47
    Stockade Centre 49
    swearing allegiance 42
Exhibition Buildings, Melbourne 32

Federation 26
    flag 6, 27
    Parliament opening 38
    star added to flag 39
Fighter Squadron 69
Flag Act, 1953 6, 38
Flags,
    Aboriginal flag 6, 52, 106
    Australian National flags
        Blue Ensign 99, 102, 103,
        Red Ensign 99, 102, 103, 108
    British flags
        Red Ensign 99
        Blue Ensign 99
        White Ensign 99
    Services
        Australian Air Force 108
        Civil Aviation 108
        Ensign 108
        Murray Rivers 108
        White Ensign 108
    States
        New South Wales 105
        Queensland 105
        South Australia 105
        Tasmania 105
        Victoria 105
        Western Australia 105
    Territories
        Australian Capital Territory 107
        Christmas and Cocos Islands 107
        Norfolk Island 107
        Northern Territory 107
        Torres Strait Islands 107
Forest Creek 43
Freeman, Cathy 12, 16

Diggers' flag 43
Dexter, Mr 44

Gallipoli 2
Gaté, Gabriel 85
Gaze, Andrew 3

Gill, Samuel Thomas 8
Governor General 33
Grand Prix 94
Grigorieva, Tatiana 91

Hanson, Pauline 76
Havelock Tobacco Company 30
Hawkins, Leslie John 34
Herald Newspaper design 97
Hewitt, Lleyton 97
Hopetoun, Countess 32
Howard, John 90

Jones, Kerry 8

Kangaroos,
    boxing flag 6, 82
    advertising symbol 82
Keating, Paul 109
Kelly, Edward, 'Ned' 51
Kelly, 'Reckless' 50
Kennedy, Russell 51
Kewpie doll greeting card 83
King Edward VII 37
King George III 20
King, Trooper John 46, 47, 50
Kipling, Rudyard 24
Kokoda 72
Korea 75

Labor Party 76
Labuan 67
Lalor, Peter 43
Lambing Flat 22
    flag 50
Leunig, Michael 18, 19, 86
Liberal Party 76
Lindsay, Norman 56

Menzies, Robert 38, 57, 70
Monarchists movement 8

National Colonial Flag for Australia,
    Nicholson and Bingle 6, 24, 26
National Flag of Australia
    adopted 36
New Zealand 77
Newstead, Victoria 98
Nuttal, Egbert John 34

Olympic Games 2000, 16
    beach volley ball 93
    Brown, George, dancer 16
    Freeman, Cathy, athlete 16
    Grigorieva, Tatiana 91
    spectators 92, 93
    opening ceremony 90
One Nation 76

Palmer, Ambrose 83
Parkes, Sir Henry 24
Paterson, Andrew 'Banjo' 26, 53
People magazine 86
Phillip, Governor Arthur 6, 20
Postcards 76, 88
Posters,
    Australia Day 85
    recruiting 5

Queen Elizabeth II 38
Queen Victoria 55

Reconciliation badge 53
Reconciliation flag 52
Red Cross 74
Red Ribbon Agitation 43
Republican Debate 6
Review of Reviews 6, 38
    competition winners 34
    flag design 32–36

Scruby, Harold 90, 107
Serious, Yahoo 50
Singapore, fall of 68
South Australia, proclamation 22
Southern Cross 6, 55
Stevens, W 34
Stoddart, Paul 95
Sydney Olympics
  (see Olympic Games)

Tanner, Les, cartoon 53
Tarakan, Borneo 65
Thailand 68
Thomas, Harold 6, 52, 106
Tobruk 67
Toys 89
Troops 55, 56
Tucker, Mark 109
Twain, Mark 77

utes 87
Union Jack 6, 100

Vasey, Major-General George 72
VE Day 73
Victoria, Queen 55
Victory Parade 74
    flags 78

Waltzing Matilda 26
War Bonds 62
Webber, Mark 95
Wentworth and Bland flag 12
White Australia Policy 50
Whitlam, Gough 10
Woolner, Thomas, sculptor 24

BIBLIOGRAPHY:
Flag of Stars. Frank Cayley. Rigby Limited, Adelaide, 1966

Land, Labour & Gold. William Howitt, Lowden Publishing, Kilmore, 1972. First published 1855

Recollections of a Bleeding Heart: A Portrait of Paul Keating PM. Don Watson, Knopf Publishing, Random House, Sydney 2002.

Newspapers
The Age, Sydney Morning Herald Bendigo Advertiser

ACKNOWLEDGEMENTS:

I would like to thank the archivists and keepers of our national heritage; The Art Gallery of New South Wales, Art Gallery of South Australia, Australian National Archives, Australian War Memorial Canberra, Ballarat Fine Art Gallery, La Trobe Library, State Library of Victoria, National Gallery of Victoria, National Library of Australia, Queen Victoria Museum Launceston, Tasmania, State Parliamentary Library, Victoria.

I would also like to acknowledge the work of Harold Scruby of Ausflag, and the hundreds of designers, artists and ordinary Australians who have contributed their own efforts to the great flag debate, some of which are included in this book.

To the cartoonists John Allison, Michael Leunig, Ron Tanberg and the late Les Tanner, all whose creative eye and critical observation have given so much joy and gentle instruction to all Australians.

Australia Post, Australian Labor Party, *People* magazine, Portal Aird Publications, Skansen Giftware and Mitch Dowd for allowing me to reproduce their products and logos. John Pasquarelli for permission to reproduce the photographs of Pauline Hansen.

Doug Mills for the loan of his Federation flag, and Russell Kennedy for his reconciliation flag, and Ralph Bartlett, secretary of the Australian Flag Association for his excellent eye, advice and assistance in previewing this book.